CULTURAL AND STRUCTURAL DIMENSIONS OF FAMILY

CULTURAL AND STRUCTURAL DIMENSIONS OF FAMILY

A Study of Jalari Fishermen

M. KODANDA RAO

CONCEPT PUBLISHING COMPANY, NEW DELHI-110059

ISBN 81-7022-270-2

First Published 1990

M. Kodanda **Rao** (*b.* 1939)

Published by
Ashok Kumar Mittal
Concept Publishing Company
A/15-16, Commercial Block, Mohan Garden
NEW DELHI-110059 (India)

Lasertypeset by
Microtech Advance Printing Systems (Pvt.) Ltd.
H-13, Bali Nagar,
NEW DELHI-110015

Printed in India by
Taj Press
DELHI-110006

DEDICATED
TO
MY MOTHER

CONTENTS

LIST OF TABLES

ACKNOWLEDGEMENTS

I would like to record my gratitude to Professor N. Subba Reddy for initiating me to the field of Anthropology and Research on whose advice I took up the study of the fishermen communities. The first four chapters of this work are the revised version of part of my doctoral dissertation. I am grateful to Professor K.V. Ramana for his guidance and encouragement in preparation of my doctoral dissertation entitled 'Family and Kinship among the Jalaris of Coastal Andhra', submitted to Andhra University, Waltair, in 1975. I am thankful to Dr. T.N. Madan, Dr. Sylvia Vatuk and the late Prof. M.S.A. Rao for inspecting the manuscript and offering valuable comments. Professor M.S.A. Rao had taken special interest and he particularly encouraged me for publication of this work. I record my gratitude to him.

I am indebted to the people of Jalaripalem for co-operating with me to understand the culture and society of the Jalaris. My debt to Mr. Kambala Bhooloka and Mr. Kasarapu Tatayya, my principal informants during my fieldwork in 1968-69 and again in 1985, is immense.

I thank Dr. Yethiraj Kumar of Andhra University for permitting me an access to his field notes of the research project on Dibbapalem Rehabilitation Centre and the research investigators of the project, Mr. and Mrs. Varma, for their assistance during my revisit to the Jalaris. I am also thankful to Mr. Nageswara Rao, Dr. Seshan, Mr. B.V. Sharma and Mr. N. Sudhakara Rao for their constant help and unfailing interest in my work.

M. KODANDA RAO

LIST OF FIGURES

ONE

INTRODUCTION

THE FOCUS of this book is the study of family and household among the Jalaris of Coastal Andhra, South India. There had been considerable neglect of intensive field studies of kinship in India (see Rivers, 1914:27 and Dumont and Pocock, 1957:44). There are, of course, a few exceptions of general studies in which kinship is discussed. The earliest of these is Srinivas work on the Coorgs (1952) in which he presented a detailed analysis of the working of the Coorg joint family. The discussion of family and kinship is very limited in scope in the subsequent works published by Dube (1955), Bailey (1957), Epstein (1962) and Beals (1962). Berreman (1963) presented an exhaustive discussion of kin groups and kinship among the Paharis of North India.

Mayer (1960), however, has published an important book on caste and kinship and his interest in kinship is confined to an analysis of the internal structure of caste. Another study of importance was authored by Ross in 1961. Though it is not an anthropological field work monograph (see Madan 1965: 1-2, Abbi, 1969: 116-8), nevertheless, it was devoted exclusively to the study of Hindu family in an urban setting.

Besides these books, however, there are several papers published, during the fifties and sixties, notably by Gough (1952; 1956; 1959; 1961a; 1961b) and Dumont (1950; 1953; 1957; 1961; 1964) which contain detailed analyses of marriage and kinship in South India. There are several others written on family and household and these include : Desai (1955; 1956; 1964), Gore (1961); Gould (1960); Kapadia (1956; 1959); Klass (1966); McCormack (1958); Madan (1962a; 1962b; 1962c), etc.

The most significant book on Indian kinship is Karve's *Kinship Organization in India* (1953). In this study, she made an attempt to relate kinship terminologies and usages, covering all the linguistic and cultural regions of the country, whereby drawing generalisations of variations in kinship patterns in different zones of the country. Though her material is not based on intensive first-hand field work (see Dumont and Pocock 1957: 44) her study is a landmark in the understanding of Indian kinship organisation.

Madan (1965: 2-3) notes the basic reason for the inadequate attention paid to intensive field studies on kinship by earlier anthropologists is their pre-occupation with the study of caste, its place in Hindu society and its uniqueness which seems to have fascinated nearly all the students of Hindu society. Some writers, however, found it difficult to separate kinship from caste. Karve, thus, for example, notes : "Every caste is endogamus. Ordinarily, one has no relatives out of one's caste group, and one's relatives are all within the caste. A part of the caste is a person's actual extended kin and the rest is his possible kin. In such circumstances, caste stands for many values realized in a family and caste loyalties are comparable to family loyalties" (1956: 55).[1] In a similar way, Dumont (1957: 7)[2] also observes : "... South Indian kinship cannot be severed from the caste system".

This realisation, however, did not result in a systematic analysis of the internal structure of the caste, but caste studies have focused their attention on inter-caste relations and the external order of the caste (see Majumdar, 1958, and Berreman, 1963). Only Gough (1956), Dumont (1957) and Mayer (1960) have tried to relate caste and kinship. For example, Gough (1956) in her studies of Kumbapettai village tried to show the differences and disparities of family and kinship relations and values between Brahmans and Adi Dravidas. Dumont (1957), on the other hand, has shown clearly how the notion of hierarchy in South India permeates and articulates in marriage alliances. However, it is Mayer (1960) who brings out caste and kinship together, relating caste to the external relations and the sub-caste to the kinship relations. He writes : "On the whole, caste membership is significant for relations with other castes and sub-caste membership for activities within the caste. In turn, these activities are in fact based on the decisions of a local kindred" Mayer 1960: 5).[3]

Madan adds that reliance on Sanskrit texts in the study of caste and kinship is another important cause for the neglect of the study of Hindu kinship. He complains that "far too many scholars have been content to translate and comment on ancient and medieval Sanskrit texts, regarding them as the perennial source from which all the jural norms and the ideals of Hindu kinship flow: (1965: 4).

Writing in 1973, Madan himself observed a change in the situation:

"During the last couple of years there has been a remarkable resurgence of interest in the study of kinship in anthropological circles round the world ... during the last year or so, about half a dozen monographs on marriage and kinship in India have been published, not to mention several other books which deal with, among other things, themselves"(134). They include Gore's *Urbanization and Family Change* (1968), Kuty's *Marriage and Kinship in an Island Society* (1972), Pocock's *Kanbi and Patidar* (1972), Vatuk's *Kinship and Urbanization* (1972), Vander Veen's *I give Thee My Daughter* (1972) and Shah's *The Household Dimension of the Family in India* (1973). Some more interesting works are published in recent years such as, Inden and Nicholas' *Bengali Kinship* (1977) and Parry's *Caste and Kinship in Kangra* (1979), among others.[4]

The present work has two aims. One is to present a systematic analysis of family and household among the Jalaris after an intensive field study. Secondly, anthropological studies of the fishermen's castes of India have been very few and whatever information is available on these castes comes from the accounts of administrators and census reports.[5] The aim of the present study, therefore, is limited and confined to provide a descriptive analysis of family and household and the fundamental processes whereby the family and household forms are generated and reproduced as well as its cultural and social structural dimensions.

The design of the present work is a result of deliberate choice and arrangement of its chapters to describe and analyse the cultural and social structural aspects of family and household among the Jalaris. Chapter Two provides the general background about the social, economic, religious and political organizations of a typical fishermen's village, named Jalaripalem, as a backdrop and the starting point for further discussion on the Jalari family and household. Chapter Three discusses cultural dimensions such as the Jalari concepts, beliefs and ideas related to family and relationships that bind the parents, children and siblings with "codes of conduct". It is through this cultural model that social action is interpreted and the natural facts such as birth and death as social events are given a form and meaning. Chapter Four discusses the composition of the Jalari household as an aspect of social structural reality. It provides an analysis of maximization of values such as joint living and separate living by married adult Jalaris. It also discusses the resultant patterns of household structures as revealed in the genealogical composition. Chapter Five, on the other hand, describes and analyses patterns of household activities besides processes of reproduction. The analysis is focussed on the cultural rules and strategies related to the aspects of inheritance, succession and division of property at the cultural as well as social structural reality levels to show how the Jalaris follow, adapt and change the rules. This includes both a description of the way things and rules are conceived as well as how really things are organized. Chapter Six, deals with the changes that have taken place in the lives of the Jalaris, in general, and the family structures in particular, during the last 16 years. Finally, the concluding chapter tries to sum up the significant features of the Jalari family and household in terms of an analytical distinction made between the cultural dimension and the social structural reality.

Field-work for the present study was carried out in two phases. The data presented in the next four chapters were based on the field-work carried out in the first phase for a period of twelve months during 1968-69 in a homogeneous Jalari caste village, Jalaripalem, 22 kms. south of Visakhapatnam Town, Andhra Pradesh, South India.[6] Several visits were made to different fishermen's villages of Visakhapatnam, Vizianagaram and Srikakulam districts for the selection of site for research. Jalaripalem village was finally selected because it is fairly isolated, traditional and true representative of the Jalaris of this region. Initially, a house was rented in the nearby Palli village and then the investigator moved into Jalaripalem. The statistical data presented in this work were obtained from the field-work conducted during the period. The second phase of field-work was carried out during the months of October and December 1985, to study the changes that have taken place during the last 16 years in the lives of the Jalaris.

Though the primary data were collected in Jalaripalem, many of the observations made in the course of the study relate to the Jalaris in general. This village was selected as the locus of the study not for making a village community study but because of the need to make intensive and extensive observations of all the Jalari households of a convenient territorial unit. Being a homogeneous caste village, Jalaripalem was found as an ideal setting for that purpose.

Further, it is expected that the present study of family and household and the related activities in a single village will be of general relevance to the Jalaris of this region. Family and household relations are generated by a set of values and social interaction which have certain regularities. Such regularities are not unique to Jalaripalem but are found in adjacent villages also. Family and kinship relations overflow the boundaries of the village and family organization constitutes the basis of the traditional Jalari society.

The primary sources of data were the Jalaris themselves. The villagers were at first suspicious. Initially, the Jalaris mistook the investigator for an official of the Fisheries Department visiting the village. They were afraid of him and thought that he would collect taxes on their boats and nets. Only in the course of this field-work, rapport with them could be established and their confidence won. Though a few of them remained suspicious and uncommunicative throughout, others became friendly and gave information freely.

The starting point of the investigations was a sociological census. All anthropological techniques of data collection were used to obtain the relevant information. Participant observation and interviewing are the chief techniques besides group discussions and informal exchanges. The other techniques used were collection of genealogies, case histories and the use of schedules. Genealogical method was used to collect data on family and household composition which were the major source of information. Case history method was used for collecting empirical data regarding real life situations. This included case studies of a number of individuals, households and events. Schedules were used for collecting data on the composition of net-groups, economic status, income and expenditure, marital status, types of families etc. The data presented on the cultural features of a Jalari family were verified and made up-to-date by brief visits to the village during 1970–1975.

REFERENCES

1. Quoted also in Madan 1965: 3.
2. *Ibid.*
3. *Ibid.*, 3-4.
4. After I have completed this work, an important work dealing with kinship and related themes was published. Dumont's *A South Indian Sub-caste* (1986).
5. Published information on the fishermen castes of coastal Andhra Pradesh is available from the works of Thurston (1909) and from Census of India (1961). The village monograph on Mufusbandar by Census of India (1961) contains a very valuable material on the Vada and Jalari castes of Srikakulam district. Besides these works, Anthropological Survey of India has launched a series of studies on fishing communities of India.
6. Though I had established contacts with Jalaripalem village as early as in 1964, I could not really settle down and carry out the field-work continuously by staying in the village. It was only in 1968 I could come back and settle in the village and do an intensive field-work.

TWO

THE SETTING

THE PRESENT study concerns the Jalari, a fishing caste of Coastal Andhra on the east coast of India. The other important fishermen castes of this area are the Vada and Palli. The State of Andhra Pradesh is situated in a tropical region between 13° N to 20° N and has a long coast-line of 600 miles (965 kms.) extending from Itchapuram, Srikakulam district to Sullurupeta, Nellore district. There are nearly 300 fishing villages on this coast with a population of over half-a-million.

This long coast-line has a wide continental shelf extending the fishing grounds to an area of about 12,000 square miles. The sea is rough on the east and surf breaks heavily upon the coast throughout the year. There are very few harbours and ports for anchoring the boats. The commercially important varieties of marine fish in this area are : sardines, white bait, jew fish, prawn, seer, mullet and pomfret. The largest catch of sardines and white bait comes from Visakhapatnam, Vizianagaram and Srikakulam, the three northern districts of the State. A variety of nets are used from fishing and are operated on stitched boats and catamarans.

The extension of the continental shelf to many miles out in the sea provides a large area suitable for marine fishing. Easy slopes of the many long sandy beaches allow boats and catamarans to be hauled up by manual labour, barring rainy season when the sea becomes very rough. Land and sea breezes in the morning and afternoon enable them to sail to and fro from the fishing grounds with the least of paddling. Fish are sufficiently abundant in this area and, despite seasonal variations, fishing is done throughout the year. The fishermen do not like to spend longer period on sea. They sail early in the morning into the sea and return by afternoon. Fishing boats do not operate usually beyond one mile from the shore and the Jalaris do not take the risk involved in deep sea fishing.

Fishermen community occupies very low social status in Hindu caste system : the Palli, Vada and Jalari are all perceived by the high caste Hindus as fishermen (*chepalvallu*) and a low hierarchical status is given to them. Fishing occupation is rated very lowly and they place fishermen practically at the bottom of the social hierarchy. Fishermen, however, are treated as clean castes and their superiority over service castes like *mangali* (barber) and *chakali* (washerman) is conceded. The untouchable castes such as the *Mala* and *Madiga*, in turn, are treated by fishermen as inferior. On their part, the fishermen castes acknowledge the superiority of all the other castes in a hierarchical order with the Brahman at the top followed by Kshatriya and Vaishya. The Jalaris maintain close and intense relations with their immediate neighbours, the Vada and Palli, in the spheres of economic, political and religious activities. Their common traditional economic pursuit brings them together with an identity of common occupation and a sense of belongingness.

A VILLAGE ON THE EAST COAST

Jalaripalem represents a typical, homogeneous Jalari caste village in Visakhapatnam district. The Visakhapatnam district has a coast-line of 100 miles (140 kms.) with 78 fishing villages with hamlets and a population of 64,703 persons. Most of the Jalaris live in this district which seems to be the place of their origin.[1] Since the village is exclusively inhabited by the Jalaris, an analysis of the village life also reveals significant features of the Jalari caste organization.[2]

The Jalaris live in villages situated on the sea coast, with natural barriers of back-waters, creeks and sand dunes which make their homes almost inaccessible during the rainy season. Such natural barriers make fishermen lose touch with the rest of the population and to some extent force them to live in isolation. Jalari villages are generally congested with overlapping of thatched huts. They lack proper communication and also basic civic amenities such as sanitation, lights, medical facilities, schools, etc.

Village boundaries are based on local usage and every village is identified with a name. A number of principles of social groupings enter into the making of this village group and its solidarity. It is a local unit in the sense that its inhabitants occupy a common territory for their habitation. The villagers have the right to use the beach adjoining their village for sailing and landing their crafts. In a way, Jalari village represents a sociological unit and its members are conscious of their membership by the name of the village which differentiates them from fellow Jalaris and other villagers of the neighbourhood.

Jalaripalem village is situated on the east coast on 17°-25" northern latitude and 82°-60" eastern longitude by the shore of Bay of Bengal. Fishing is the main economic activity. Being fairly well-connected to the upland tract, this is one of the few fishing villages that supply fish regularly to the neighbouring villages and the town.

The nearest industrial and commercial centre is Visakhapatnam Town, 15 miles north of the village. However, the contacts of the fishermen with the town are limited and only a few fisherwomen go to the town market to trade fish and return to the village by night. For the purchase of domestic requirements, the villagers go mostly to Balacheruvu a market place at a distance of three miles, and a *shandy* which meets every Monday.

Jalaripalem has an area of less than a square mile bounded by Pedametta (a Palli caste village) on the south-west and Gangavaram (a Vada caste village) on the south. On its northern side at a distance of one mile, Jalaripalem is separated from another village Dibbapalem by a backwater stream Balacheruvu *Upputeru* (See Fig. 2.1).

The land surface of the village gently slopes from east to west and north to south. The Balacheruvu *Upputeru,* the samll stream is full of water during tide and rainy season. There is a sandy tract of less than a furlong in-between the village and the sea. Towards the south-west, at the end of the small stream of backwaters, there is a pedestrian path leading to Pedametta and Nellimukku villages and there are *mogali* (screwpine) trees obviously planted to prevent soil erosion. This marks the beginning of agricultural fields, cultivated mostly by the Palli and Golla caste people of Pedametta and Chinametta villages. Thus, the area to the south-west of the village is full of agricultural fields with wells for irrigation. Jalari women go to these wells to fetch water for drinking purpose.

Jalaripalem is built on the edge of sand slopes and bounded by backwaters on the north and the west. The sand tract in-between the village and sea-shore is called *karavaka* where the fishermen dry and repair their fishing nets in the afternoons.

The village is surrounded by some stray palmyra trees and causurina plantations. Causurina plantations are abundant in this area bordering the portion of sandy tract near the sea-shore. The south-western part of the village is inhabited by agriculturists. While the fisherman community finds the eastern part of the sandy tract

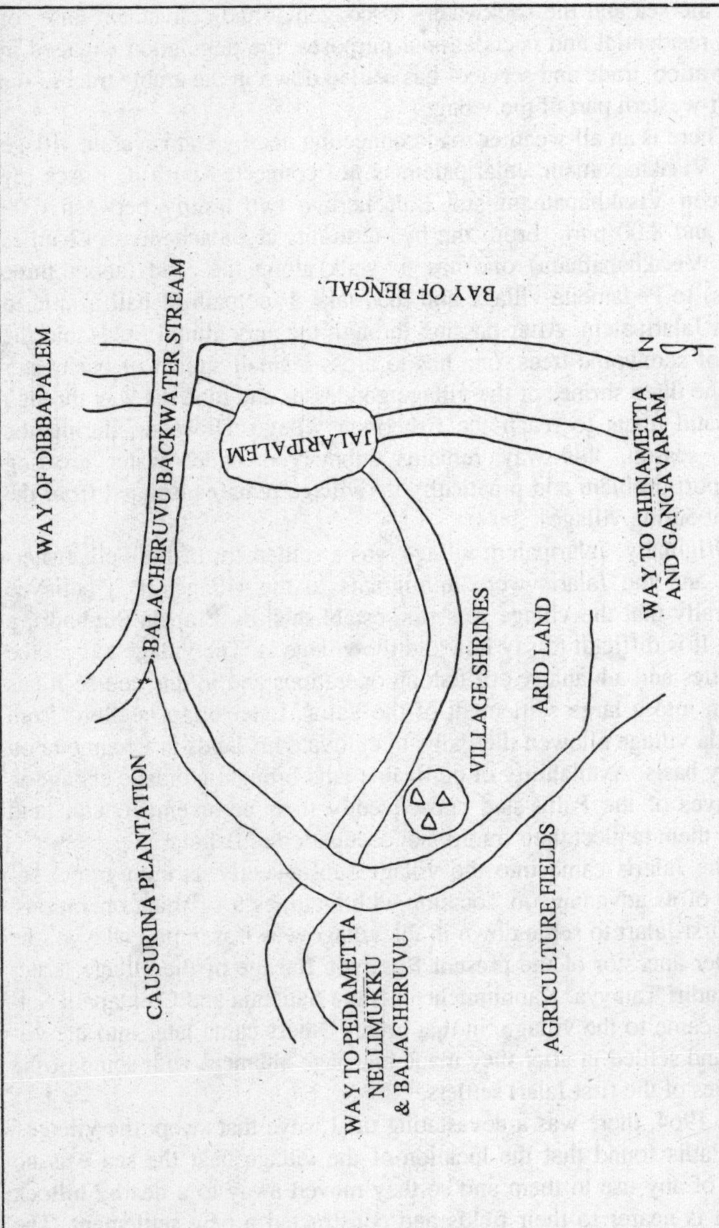

FIG. 2.1 : *Location of Jalaripalem Village*

near the sea and the backwaters as congenial and convenient base for their residential and occupational purposes, the population engaged in cultivation, trade and services has settled down in the arable tract in the south-western part of the village.

There is an all-weather road connecting nearby Gangavaram village with Visakhapatnam. Jalaripalem is not connected with it. Buses ply between Visakhapatnam and Balacheruvu two hourly between 6.00 a.m. and 8.00 p.m.[3] From the bus terminus at Balacheruvu (12 miles from Visakhapatnam) one has to walk along the road (about three miles) to Pedametta village and then take a footpath of half a mile to reach Jalaripalem. After passing through the agricultural fields and the row of screwpine trees, one has to cross a small stream of backwater and the three shrines of the village goddesses and plod his way through the sand tracts to reach the fisherman village. However, during the rainy season, this way remains submerged under water creating transport problem and practically the village remains isolated from the neighbouring villages.

Originally, Jalaripalem village was a settlement of the Palli fishermen, and the Jalaris were immigrants to the village. It is believed generally that the village was first established by Erabala Simhadri, a Palli. It is difficult to say how old the village is. The village has all the facilities and advantages of fishing operations and in due course it has grown into a large settlement of the Pallis. Later on, a landlord from Yarada village allowed the Pallis to cultivate his lands in Pedametta on timely basis. Availability of cultivable land brought a drastic change in the lives of the Pallis and consequently their involvement with land made them neglect their traditional occupation of fishing.

The Jalaris came into the village subsequently as immigrants because of its advantageous location with facilities for fishing operations. The first Jalari to settle down in the village was Kasarapu Pedayya, the founder ancestor of the present Kasarapu lineage of the village. Later on, Kadiri Tatayya, Kantumuchchu Nalla Sattenna and Chintapalli Sattenna came to the village, in that order. Others came later into the village and settled in after they made marriage alliances with some of the families of the first Jalari settlers.

In 1964, there was a devastating tidal wave that swept the village.[4] The Pallis found that the location of the village near the sea was no more of any use to them and so they moved away to a nearby hillock which is nearer to their fields and constructed a new settlement. The present Palli settlement, called Pedametta, is situated half a mile to the south-west of Jalaripalem, beyond the agricultural fields. The Jalaris, on the other hand, despite heavy loss of property and lives in that disastrous tidal wave stayed in the original village for its advantageous location.

Presently, Jalaripalem is a homogeneous Jalari village with a total population of 380 individuals who live in 77 households. Table 2.1 shows the distribution of the village population age-wise (in the year 1969).

Men are usually engaged in fishing while women do the selling of fresh and cured fish in the nearby market places. There are 127 (30.7 per cent) active fishermen engaged exclusively in marine fishing. They are in the age-groups of 15 to 55 years. Individuals below 15 years and above 55 years are not considered as active fishermen. However, boys in the age-group of 12 to 15 years and some older men are occasionally recruited into the big-net groups, but they cannot be construed as active fishermen. They are usually employed for minor jobs in the big-net fishing operations.

The population of Jalaripalem is divided into nine named descent groups (*intiperulu*) and represents 10 lineages which are local descent groups with corporate activities of their own. Each such

Table 2.1: Distribution of the Population of Jalaripalem Age-wise

Age Group	*Frequency*	*Percentage*
1-5	20	5.3
6-10	49	12.9
11-15	49	12.9
16-20	55	14.5
21-25	37	9.7
26-30	21	5.5
31-35	24	6.3
36-40	30	7.9
41-45	30	7.9
46-50	12	3.2
52-55	23	6.1
56-60	6	1.6
61-65	16	4.2
66-70	5	1.3
71-75	3	0.8
Total Population	380	100.0

lineage represents the interests of several households which are agnatically related to each other and whose genealogical relations are traceable through a common ancestor. The household is the basic unit of the Jalari social organization which consists of patrilineally related kinsmen, their unmarried female agnates and wives. Table 2.2 shows the distribution of households among the 10 lineage groups in the village.

Table 2.2: Distribution of Households by Lineages

	Name of Lineage	*No. of Households*
1.	Kadiri	20
2.	Kasarapu	8
3.	Kantumuchchu (Senior)	13
4.	Kantumuchchu (Junior)	6
5.	Chintapalli	9
6.	Nolli	6
7.	Kambala	2
8.	Karuku	6
9.	Vadamodili	2
10.	Mdou	5
	Total	77

All the descent groups of the village are equal in status, except the Kadiri lineage which enjoys superior status in the village organization and whose lineage head is the recognized head of the village.[5] Since the Kadiri lineage performs a special function in village administration, it is considered higher in status over the other descent groups of the village. The village headman commands prestige because of his position and power in the village.

All the lineage heads of the village enjoy higher status and prestige in the village and are equal to one another. They are the recognized leaders of the village and are called as the "elders of the village" (*grama peddalu*). Although economic disparity among the Jalaris is not conspicuous, the owners of boats and net-groups enjoy relatively superior status and prestige and are referred to by their crew as the "big-men" (*pedda manisulu*). The pattern of settlement in the village clearly shows that the household of agnatic kinsmen occupy a contiguous area for common habitation in the village.[6] The households of patrilineal kin tend to cluster around a common habitation area, defined exclusively as belonging to their ancestors. Each cluster of such households constitutes a distinct grouping in the village and is known as *veedhi* (a street). Each such street is named after the local descent group that lives in that area. There are 10 such habitation areas or streets for all the lineages, representing the nine named descent groups of the village (see Fig. 2.2)

Scattering of the households of agnatic kinsmen from their usual habitation area in the village may also take place if there are dissensions and factions among the agnates. The division of the Kantumuchchu descent group of Jalaripalem into two independent and separate lineages had its effect on the settlement pattern in the village. The households belonging to the junior lineage moved farther south. Differences with uncles and cousins made Kadiri Kistamma to move away from the usual habitation area of his natal household to farther east. People who fall sick may be told by the local astrologer or by the *dasudu* (village priest) to change the place of residence. When tidal waves swept away some of the houses of Kasarapu lineage, whose settlement was nearer to the sea and backwaters, they moved away and built their new houses further west, thus extending usual habitation area of their local descent group. But, on the whole, the pattern is that a number of agnatically related households of a descent group live together in a separate site of its own in the village and is traditionally recognized as a street belonging to that local descent group.

Within the village there is a dual organisation based on territorial division, locally known as the *undi* system. Such territorial division of caste in a village is a widespread system of social organisation not only confined to the Jalaris, but also reported as existing in other castes of this region.[7] The system of dual organisation in the village is based on territorial division and has no significance to the kinship and marriage system of the villagers.

In Jalaripalem, the village territory is divided broadly into two divisions, known as *ega veedhi* (Upper Ward) and *diga veedhi* (Lower Ward). The Upper Ward consists of the local descent groups inhabiting the northern part of the village and the Lower Ward consists of the descent groups inhabiting the southern part of the village (see Fig. 2.2). For the descent groups of the Upper Ward, Kasarapu Tatayya (head of Kasarapu lineage) is the recognized leader, while for the descent groups of the Lower Ward, Kadiri Krishna Murthy of Kadiri lineage (the village headman) is the recognized leader. All the descent groups distribution of the lineage of the village into two divisions. of the village belong to either of these two groups. Table 2.3 shows the distribution of the lineage of the village into two divisions.

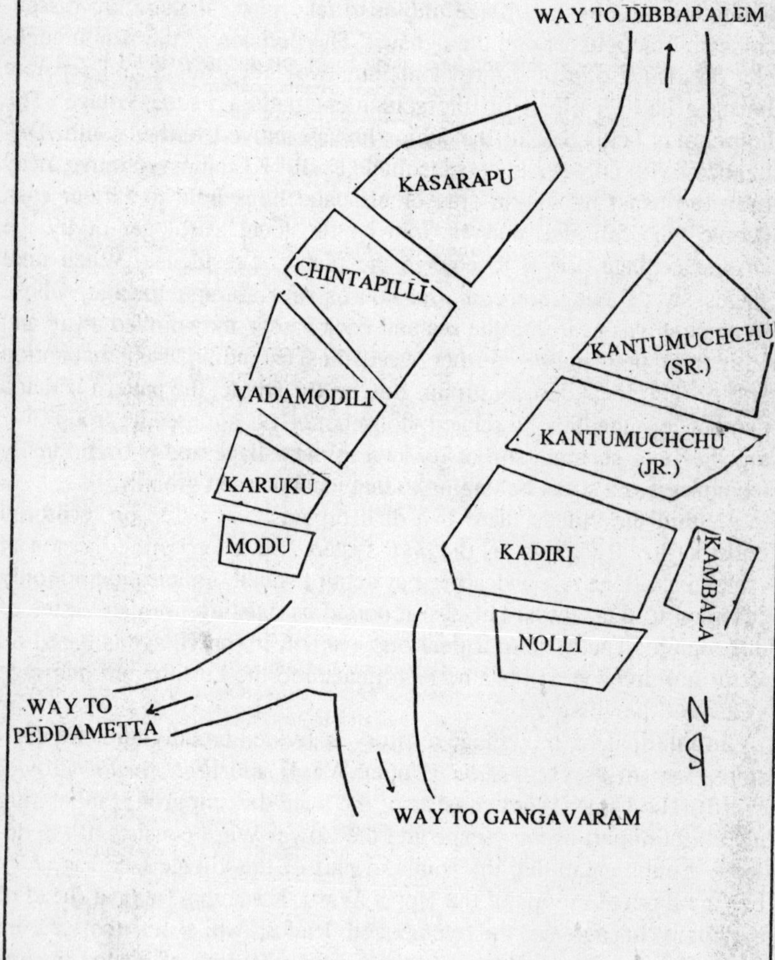

FIG. 2.2 : *Pattern of Settlement of the Village*

Table 2.3: Division of Local Descent Groups into Dual Organization in Jalanpalem Village

Upper Ward	*Lower Ward*
Kasarapu	Kadiri
Chintapilli	Kantumuchchu (Senior)
Vadamodili	Kantumuchchu (Junior)
Karuku	Nolli
Modu	Kambala

It was said that the first settlers of the village occupied the northern and southern parts of the village and built up their houses, each facing the other. When Kasarapu Peddayya, the first Jalari immigrant into the village, settled in the northern part of the village, the next immigrant into the village, Kadiri Tatayya, occupied the southern part of the village and built his house. The Jalaris who immigrated later into the village settled and constructed their households adjoining these two main settlements of Kadiri and Kasarapu descent groups. These later immigrants are close relatives of these two early settlers and according to the closeness and intimacy of their relations with the first settlers they chose to occupy either of these two sites of the village.

It is necessary to realize that members of each division have a strong feeling of 'unity' among themselves than they have with those of the opposing division. Households belonging to one division of the village consult its leader on marriage negotiation and other important occasions related to social control.[8] For example, during marriages, all the members belonging to one division help their fellow member who is celebrating the marriage and construct the marriage *pandal* and render all the help that is needed on that occasion. The head of the household, performing the marriage ceremony, invites all the members of the households of his division for marriage dinner, but invites only one person from each of the households of the opposing division. This dual organization is also manifested in the dinner arrangements they make for the members of these two divisions. All the members of one division sit together in a row, opposite to the members of the other division who sit in another row. This pattern is also seen in birth and death ceremonies where the members of a particular division are given prominence and importance over members of the opposing division. When a girl belonging to one division reaches puberty, the ceremony is first attended by members of that division and they are the first to present *sare* (presentation of clothes and fruits) to the girl; others are expected to visit the girl later.

ECONOMIC ARRANGEMENTS AND CONTRACTS

The Economic life of the people of Jalaripalem is sustained by fishing and related activities with explicitly defined economic transactions and contracts. Unlike the Vadas and Pallis the Jalaris do not engage themselves in agriculture. They do not own any cultivable land and have no interests in agriculture. All the households of Jalaripalem depend entirely on fishing for their livelihood. There are two categories of economic arrangements and contracts in the form of membership in various net-groups organised for fishing operations in different seasons. These arrangements and contracts form the basis of the village economic life whereby Jalari households exist as viable economic units.

Every Jalari household and its adult male members are members of a *pedola* (big-net group) of their local descent group. Big-net fishing activities are a common economic enterprise of a local descent group among the Jalaris. Big-net operations are carried on from October to February when commercially important fish like *kavvallu* (sardines) and *neththallu* (white bait) are available in abundance. For fishing a big-net group must have an adequate labour force of at least 20 active adult fishermen for conducting fishing operations. Therefore, the local descent groups are the automatic choice for organizing a big-net group as they provide the necessary labour force as well as an assured security for the future for such a large scale fishing operation. Each local descent group thus organizes its own big-net and all the adult members of a local descent group become the crew of the net-group whereby every adult male and its household is involved in its economic activity.

The fact that the crew of a big-net group consists of only kinsmen of a local descent group, agnatically related to each other, gives continuity both to economic and social relations. Every Jalari has a right to work in big-net fishing of his local descent group by virtue of his birth and descent rights. As such, every Jalari adult in the village invariably belongs to one of the big-net groups of his local descent group and one's livelihood is assured in this pattern. This also benefits the participating individuals and their households with an assured security.

This pattern also provides greater stability to the net-group composition and eliminates uncertainties involved in securing the necessary labour force for big-net fishing activity for every season.

Economic relations among members of a net-group are always regarded as partnership among equals of shared interests around a corporation. The rights over a big-net as a rule belong to a single local descent group and all its households claim equal rights of ownership over its big-net and fishing activity. However, such a notion of equality of control of rights is theoretical. In practice, only the senior households of local descent group control exclusive rights over the eight parts (*arapa*) of a big-net while the participation of the members of other households, on the basis of genealogical rights, is a symbolic representation of the unity of a local descent group.

When a local descent group does not have the required labour force of its own, it makes certain economic adjustments with a like descent group, either by allocating some rights of ownership to it or by joining such a local descent group with rights of ownership in its big-net. Where the available labour force is inadequate in the village, fishermen are recruited from the neighbouring villages as share-croppers (*raithulu*) without any rights of ownership. Table 2.4 shows the composition of big-net groups in Jalaripalem and the adjustments they make with the other households and lineages which do not have big-nets of their own.

Big-net fishing is carried on only seasonally for about five months and the institutional arrangements for big-net activity provide only partial security to one's economic pursuit and to the sustenance of his household. As fish become scarce in the off-shore, big-net fishing is abandoned in preference to smaller net-groups consisting of two to eight persons. Therefore, besides big-net groups the Jalaris are compelled to organize themselves into smaller net-groups to continue fishing activity both during the off-shore fishing season and in the non-fishing season.

The Jalaris continue their fishing activity either by organizing net-groups independently or by joining a smaller net-group using small boats, catamarans and nets of different types. When a household has the necessary fishing equipment to organize a net-group of its own, one or several of its members serve as crew of the net-group. Where the household does not possess the required equipment and labour force to organize a net-group of its own, the head of the household makes other arrangements.

Table 2.4: Composition of Big-net Groups in Jalaripalem

Name of the lineage with a big-net	*No. of persons belong to the lineage of big-net*	*Name of the other lineage or its households with rights of ownership*	*No. of persons from Descent group*	*No. of persons as share-croppers*	*Total Number*
1. Kadiri	30	Nil	Nil	Nil	30
2. Kasarapu	16	Nil	Nil	10	26
3. Kantumuchchu (Senior)	25	Nil	Nil	4	29
4. Kantumuchchu (Junior)	12	Kambala	7	Nil	25
5. Chintapilli	20	Vadamodili	6	Nil	26
6. Modu	10	Nolli	8	3	23
7. Karuku	10	Kadiri*	4	8	22
Total	123	---	25	25	181

* One of the two households of Kadiri lineage is included into the big-net of Karuku lineage only after the consent of the elders of Kadiri lineage, as a short term arrangement, to relieve the pressure on its net-group which has a crew of the maximum number of fishermen. Whereas, the other household joined the big-net group of Karuku lineage on its own, and was not approved by the fellow Kadiri households.

Such arrangements can be made by joining a net-group organized by a person, who owns the necessary fishing equipment, as a share-cropper. The relationship between the net-boss (*sonth- adarudu*) of a net-group and his share-cropper (*raithu*) is based on a general understanding whereby the former gets one-third of a day's total catch as rent for his fishing equipment, while the crew of the net-group retains the remaining catch and divides it equally among all the working fishermen. Owner's share of the toal net catch, however, may seem to be excessive. But the significant factor involved in the allotment of one-third of the total net catch to the owner as rent for the use of his fishing equipment is an explicit recognition of his willingness to take the risks involved in sea fishing in this area. The rough nature of the sea, rocky paths and shallow waters are potential hazards in losing one's nets while fishing on the sea.

The understanding between the owner of the net-group and the fishermen workers is valid for only one season. The owner has an exclusive right to engage them in fishing even during the big-net fishing operations. Each such contract is renewable at the end of every season. The owner fixes the crew of his net-group right before the beginning of fishing season by paying Rs. 50 or more to each working fishermen as an advance according to the needs of each individual. However, the employees are free to leave him whenever they are dissatisfied with his net-group.

The partners in such contracts are not necessarily one's own close kin, except in the case of a net-group consisting of the personnel of a household. However, in a few cases where the partners are not close kin, affinal relations are established, in the course of time, between members working on a net-group, but they are of minimal significance to a net-group. The relationships between the partners, whether related or not, are based on explicit economic considerations and are, therefore, contractual in nature. Considerations of nearness of kinship seem to be irrelevant to the composition of small net-groups that go for deep sea fishing. While married sons with separate households of their own initially tend to remain with the net-groups of their fathers, but they are free to leave at any time. There are no apparent regularities in the kinship composition of such small net-groups in the village. Wherever the close kin are taken into a net-group, their relations are primarily determined and mostly based upon economic considerations rather than on kinship relations.

On reaching the shores of the village with their catch, fishermen reserve some portion of fish for charity and domestic consumption. The remaining fish is sold on the shore itself to contractors and retail traders. Contractors engage themselves in wholesale trade of dry fish and export them to towns within as well as outside the State. They come to the village before the start as well as during the big-net season to purchase fish. Usually, they enter into agreements with a few net-groups by advancing loans to the owners of these net-groups who, in return, are obliged to sell regularly their catch to these contractors.

Some Jalari women of the village also engage themselves in fish trade mainly acting as middlemen between the fishermen and the retail traders. They are known as *marakathelu*. The retail traders (*berakathelu*) also come from other fishing villages in the neighbourhood. These retail traders are all women; known to the middlemen and the fishermen of the village. In almost all cases, fish is sold to them on credit. In some cases, however, half of the price is paid and the remaining is paid the next morning.

When a fisherman returns to the shore with reasonably good catch, he is in the habit of taking some fish to home. When fish is brought home in the afternoon, usually the older women of the household take them to nearby markets. If the catch is more than they could sell and if they want to preserve the fish by drying, the young woman members of the household clean the fish. The scales and stomach portions are removed and processed in an earthen vessel with salt. The next day, the soaked or fermented fish is removed and dried in sun. In case of large fish, it is kept in salt water for three days and then dried in sun for about three days.

RELIGIOUS INSTITUTIONS

Jalari Village life shows a richness of ritual activities and its influence on the actions of the villagers. Their religious institutions are closely connected with the important features of their social organization. The Jalaris consider themselves Hindus. Though the villagers propitiate occasionally and worship Gods of the great tradition, their religious life is dominated by the local village and lineage deities.[9] The Jalaris may go on pilgrimages occasionally to popular Hindu religious centres as Simhachalam and Tirupathi. But the impact of Hinduism and its Gods is rather negligible.

The Jalaris believe in female deities whom they call as *ammoru* (the mother goddess). There are various female deities associated and identified with different situations and believed to control the phenomena. At the village community level, the people of Jalaripalem have four village deities who are called *peddammorlu* or *urammorlu*.

The Jalaris believe that village deities protect them from evils, epidemics and from natural disasters such as storms and tidal waves and work towards the welfare and prosperity of the villagers. The other female deities belong to the lineages of the village. They are known as *intammoru* representing each lineage. Propitiation and worship of these lineage deities are closely related with their economic organization which is based on lineage organization.

There are two kinds of religious functionaries associated with these deities in every Jalari village. One is called *dasudu*, the chief worshipper of a village deity, and the other is called *bhakthudu*, the chief worshipper of a lineage deity. *Dasudu* serves the interests of all the villagers whereas the *bhakthudu* serves only the interests of his lineage group.

Dasudu plays an important role in the village's magico-religious life and his services are constantly sought by the villagers in distress and difficulties. Whenever they wish to find an explanation for their domestic troubles and diffculties, the villagers approach one of the *dasullu* of the village. *Dasudu* employs a technique called *chupu* which has a magico-religious form and content. Through employing *chupu* technique, *dasudu* identifies the phenomena and finds out the casual relationship for all the troubles and difficulties of the villagers who approach him for help.

There are, in all, four village-deities in Jalaripalem village with one *dasudu* attached to each of these.[10] The position of priesthood is hereditary and a variety of rigid rules and regulations are prescribed for strict observation by the *dasudu* in his day-to-day life. These include refraining from sexual life, and fasting at the time of ceremonies and rituals. One comes to occupy this position of *dasudu* when he, member of the hereditary family, gets possessed by the spirit of the particular deity in a special ceremony performed in deciding the successor to the deceased chief worshipper of that particular deity. Male members of the family of the deceased *dasudu*, that is, only his sons and brothers, are considered. Table 2.5 contains the names of the village deities and their respective chief worshippers (*dasullu*) in Jalaripalem.

Table 2.5: The Village Deities and their Dasullu in Jalaripalem

Name of the Village Deity	*Name of Dasudu*
Polamma	Kasarapu Danayya
Durgamma	Kadiri Durgayya
Paidithallamma	Kantumuchchu Bangari
Bhoolokamma	Chintapilli Ammoru

Polamma is the principal deity of the village and the villagers believe her as the eldest sister of the village deities. She has no separate shrine of her own and the people of Jalaripalem believe that *grama sadanu*, (central place of the village) is the abode of their principal village deity. This place is considered sacred. The remaining three village deities have separate shrines of their own, situated at the outskirts of the village on way to Pedametta and Nellimukku villages. The village deities are housed in three small thatched huts.

The principal village deity is not symbolized in any idol form. However, at the time of village festival, it is symbolized in three small earthern pots decorated with turmeric powder (*pasupu*), vermillion (*kumkum*) and sandal paste (*gandham*) and placed in the central place of the village under the neem tree, the other three village deities, on the other hand, are symbolized in idol forms made of neem wood. They are painted with colours and decorated with silk dresses and ornaments. All these three deities hold a sword coated in silver in the left hand. Villagers perform the village festivals once in three years and these idols are painted and decorated and made ready for such occasions.

The village festival lasts for three days and on the last evening, four goats are sacrificed in the name of each village deity. All the festivals are conducted during the month of May, i.e., at the end of active fishing season.

The festival is celebrated in the name of the four village deities. It begins with worship of the principal deity, Polamma. All the villagers, their relatives and friends from the neighbouring villages join together for the celebration. Funds required for the festival are raised by the village elders and are kept with Kasarapu Danayya, *dasudu* of the principal village deity, Polamma. Subscriptions are usually collected from each household on the basis of the number of married adult males. The elders of the village decide details of the festival in a meeting attended by all the four religious functionaries.

VILLAGE ADMINISTRATION

Jalaripalem, traditionally, has been an autonomous unit administered through its village headman and village elders. The headman and the council of elders are drawn from different segments of the population of the village. Since Jalaripalem is homogeneous in its caste composition, the village council which represents the respective lineages of the village, is a caste council itself.[11]

The headman of Kadiri lineage of the village, Kadiri Krishna Murthy, is the recognized headman of the village. He is called *grama pedda* (village headman) or *kula pedda* (caste headman). The headman holds office through a socially recognized hereditary right, invested in Kadiri lineage and its senior family. Headmanship passes from the senior member of that family to the next senior member, that is, to a son or a brother.

The headman in a Jalari village is an influential person. He plays a dominant role in village administration and in its organisation and is the central figure in the village activities. He also represents the village in its external relations and acts as a spokesman for his village. However, the position of village headman is titular and he cannot be considered as a powerful man exercises political authority with various social and economic advantages. He is a social and economic representative of the village and its council of elders. The Jalari political system provides limited economic advantages or authority to the village headman. However, a powerful man always wields greater authority than a weak figure.

The caste council has full jurisdiction over the village intra-family relations, neighbourhood relations, matters related to marriage, community festivals, social control and other related social matters and its relations with neighbouring villages. Whenever any problem is brought to the notice of the village headman by an aggrieved party, the matter is circulated through *sammiti*, his executive assistant, to other members of the council of elders. The concerned parties are informed through *sammiti* to attend the meeting of the village council. The next morning, *sammiti* brings the parties to central place of the village (*grama sadanu*) where the meeting is conducted. In the same way, other members of the village council are brought to the meeting place. All the members of the village council are informed and are made acquainted with details of the case. On the basis of the opinion of the members, the village headman gives his judgement.

The cases that come before the village council of elders are both civil and criminal. Civil cases are related to domestic affairs, such as disputes between wife and husband, elopements and divorce and of property and inheritance. Criminal cases are disputes involving fights. In all the cases, the guilty persons are levied fines which range from Rs. 10 to 50. Fines are to be paid to the aggrieved party in some cases and in other cases to the community itself. The village elders are also paid a sum of money by both the parties which is spent on drinking liquor. Serious cases like murders are reported to government officials at Nellimukku.

The offices of the village headman, his assistant and the council of elders of the village are hereditary and the term of office is usually for life unless the conduct of the member is very bad. The present village headman is very powerful and influential. The other prominent and influential persons of the village council of elders are Kasarapu Tatayya and Kambala Bhooloka.

Though Jalaripalem is an autonomous social unit by itself, it has always been part of the wider political and administrative system of the region. For administrative purposes, Jalaripalem is an integral part of Nellimukku revenue village.[12] Two government officials, Munsiff and *Karanam*, are located in Nellimukku. The village Munsiff, a Reddi, is responsible for maintenance of law and order in Nellimukku revenue village. The village *Karanam* belongs to karanam caste, an Oriya-speaking caste. His duties include keeping accounts and records pertaining to land ownership, land utilization, crop pattern, assessment and collection of land tax, registration of births and deaths, etc. The villagers of Jalaripalem have limited contacts with the village *Karanam* since they have no cultivable land in their possession and the only contacts they have are when they report to the *Karanam* of the births and deaths in the village. On the other hand, the leaders of the village council maintain occasional contacts with the village Munsiff as and when there are inter-village disputes and cases of murder in the village. On the whole, the Jalaris have very limited contacts with the government officials because of the nature of their economic activity. Even in cases related to law and order the people of Jalaripalem rarely go for a settlement to the village Munsiff or to the village *Karanam*. The Jalaris do not take their disputes to government officials even if they are not satisfied with the decision and judgement of the village council of elders.

The introduction of *Panchayat Raj* (a system of democratic decentralization) with Nellimukku village as headquarters of Nellimukku village *panchayat*, covering as many as 13 villages and hamlets including Jalaripalem village, has not changed the political situation and the traditional leadership pattern in the village.[13] The village is still an autonomous unit administered by its headman and the council of elders.

Jalaripalem is entitled to send a representative to Nellimukku village panchayat to represent its people. But, it has never shown any interest in the new system of democratic decentralization and the village is being represented by an outsider from Nellimukku village. *Panchayat Raj* system has no significant impact on the leadership pattern of the village and the traditional system remains undisturbed.

REFERENCES

1. Thurston (1909) refers to four original towns of the Jalari caste which are situated in Visakhapatnam District (1909:443).
2. Numerous field studies considered the village as a principal unit for understanding the Indian Society. However Dumont and Pocock (1957: 25-32; 1960: 88-89) doubted the significance of the village either as a corporate group or as a useful

unit for analysis. Such doubts can be resolved if the village under study is a homogeneous caste village.

3. Later on a direct city bus was introduced plying from Visakhapatnam to Gangavaram every day for every two hours.
4. This disastrous tidal wave is still remembered and talked about by the older people of the coastal villages of Andhra who heard it from their parents and grand parents. It is popularly known as the disastrous tidal wave (*bandaru uppena*) that submerged Bandar town, then a flourishing port in Krishna district.
5. Kadiri lineage is accorded higher status among the Jalaris throughout this region and traditionally the headmen of most of the Jalari villages belong to this lineage. In Jalaripalem, for instance, members of Kasarapu descent are the first settlers in the village. But soon after the arrival of Kadiri people the position of headman of the village was bestowed upon its senior member (see Kodanda Rao 1973: 17-18).
6. The residential pattern of a village in this region to some extent is structure of the village in which particular caste groups or lineages tend to reside in separate sections whereby maintaining their physical and social distinctiveness according to their rank and economic status. (See Mandelbaum 1972: 340-41).
7. Ramana (1971: 97) notes the functioning of such "undis" among some caste groups in Visakhapatnam town. Similarly Lynch notes in his work on Agra: "functionally, a *thok* is a unit of social control, commensality, co-operation and effective relationships" (1969: 182).
8. The leaders of the lineages of these two opposing divisions protect the interests of their respective members in the village panchayat. Likewise, the leaders of these two divisions support the lineage heads belonging to their respective divisions in the village council.
9. Redfield (1956) recognizes the differences between a great tradition and a little tradition which are inter-dependent. "In a civilization there is a great tradition of the reflective few, and there is a little tradition of the largely unreflective many. The great tradition is cultivated in schools or temples; the little tradition works itself out and keeps itself going in the lives of the unlettered in their village communities". (41-42).
10. These four village deities are the principal lineage deities of the original Jalari settlers of the village. However festivals and celebrations to these deities are performed collectively by all the villagers as a common expression of the village solidarity.
11. The village panchayat is called either as *grama panchayithi* (village council) or *kula panchayithi* (caste council). "A panchayat is a means of gathering, consolidating and giving effect to public opinion" (Mandelbaum 1972: 370).
12. A revenue village is an administrative unit of several villages. Several such revenue villages comprise a taluk and several taluks comprise a district. In each revenue village, the government appoints its village officials, namely, *Karanam* and Munsiff.
13. Panchayati Raj system, a democratic decentralization, was introduced to involve the villagers in the task of rural reconstruction to organize village panchayats and to endow them to function as units of self-government, Nellimukku panchayat has a provision to elect nine panchayat members. Several village panchayats constitute a Panchayat Samithi. Panchayati Raj system consists of three-tier development agency, the panchayat at village level, the panchayat samithi at the block level; and zilla parishad at the district level.

THREE

CONCEPTS AND MEANINGS

TTHE CULTURAL dimension of the Jalari family discussed in this chapter includes the Jalari concepts, beliefs and ideas binding the parents, children, siblings and ancestors that create and reveal relationships of solidarity between the individuals, both living and dead, and the family with 'codes of conduct'. The ideas, concepts and beliefs not only guide the actions of the Jalari but are interpreted to the action to give form and meaning and to some extent instrumental in generating behaviour. The Jalari perceives the solidarity relations between parents, siblings and ancestors as emanating from an individual's birth and 'incorporation' into the family and household. These relationships bind the individual and his family with 'codes of conduct' as revealed in the passage of life. This chapter, therefore, discusses the relevant concepts, beliefs and ideas those having to do with an individual's birth and 'incorporation' into the family and the 'code of conduct' : a cultural construct of the Jalaris which is a way of perceiving reality, guiding a partly ordered complex of ongoing events and transactions into an ordered construction of social reality.

Incorporation into the Family

The process of incorporation into the family among the Jalaris consists of a series of rituals. The customary and usual modes and basis for incorporation into the family and recruitment to the household among the Jalaris are birth, adoption and marriage.[1] It is by birth which becomes central symbolic action for the process of incorporation, it does not automatically ensure the body a place into the family. The physical facts of birth as a precondition enables an individual to get incorporated into the family, while adoption is considered as a substitute to birth. On the other hand, marriage is a principle whereby a woman is recruited and incorporated into her husband's household. Thus the concepts, beliefs and ideas associated with the processes of incorporation into the family by birth, adoption and marriage, though differ significantly from each other, nevertheless bind the individuals and the families with certain codes of conduct. The concept of birth, considered as natural fact, is an ascribed status, based on the beliefs and ideas of patrilineal descent which is permanent or made permanent with morally and jurally binding rights and obligations. On the other hand, marriage is an achieved status among the Jalaris which can be terminated or changed or recreated as it is based on the principle of affinity.

On birth or adoption, a Jalari is brought into a complex network of culturally defined relationships between members of the family, his kinsmen and ancestors with morally binding obligations. Such a cultural network forms the basic framework to guide one's behaviour, to interpret one's experience and reconstruct the reality. It also culturally binds the individual not only with members of his family, but also with his family and its ancestors. Thus birth acquires significance and importance in the lives of Jalari fishermen and is expressed in beliefs and ideas related to child birth.

Pregnancy and Associated Beliefs

Pregnancy is considered a happy and fortunate event not only in the life of a woman, but also to the family to which she is recruited. The Jalaris believe that conception occurs through release of seminal fluid of the husband and the newly born child's life is made wholly out of the man alone. Consequently, they hold that children belong to man and not to the woman.

This emphasis on agnatic relationship with child-birth has implications for a male child, as patrilineal descent ensures a son with social position in the society to direct his economic, political and religious life. A man derives his rights of property inheritance, his family and lineage membership as well as his political and ritual status from his father.

However, supernatural forces are believed to prevent conception and its safe delivery. The Jalaris believe that ancestors of the family would come back to earth and reborn in their households to help their sons. Thus, every birth among fishermen is a reincarnation of the ancestors of the family. As the newly born child is exposed to the wrath of evil spirits, deities of the lineage of a family are expected to protect the child from evil spirits. Ceremonies are, therefore, performed both during pregnancy and after child birth. Not only evil spirits do harm to the life of the child, but the deities of the lineage can also cause harm in the form of miscarriages. This favour or wrath of the deities of the lineage or blessings of the ancestors or the malevolence of evil spirits are believed to be the ultimate determinants for a couple to have many, some or no children and whether to have boys or girls.

The Jalaris believe that birth of a male child is auspicious and, therefore, greatly desired.[2] Besides ensuring continuity and stability of the family, it also gives a sense of security. Therefore, any number of sons are welcome to a Jalari family.

But daughters are not so welcome because they are considered as 'someone else's property' (*parayi sottu*) to be handed over to them at proper time. They are regarded as guests in the natal family. Giving them away to another family in marriage involves responsibilities on the part of parents and the family, besides creating affinal alliances. The reputation of parents and family depends on her conduct and behaviour in her husband's family. Any act of misconduct adversely reflects upon her natal household. However, despite all these responsibilities and uncertainties involved in having daughters, they regard daughters as ornaments to the family and to the fulfilment of their life. Children of both sexes are treated alike by the Jalaris.

Pregnancy and Childbirth

Pregnancy is ascertained and associated with the stoppage of the monthly menstrual course. When menstruation stops after certain period of married life, a Jalari woman considers that she is pregnant. The local expression for conception is *nelathappadam*.

When a woman experiences stoppage of menstrual blood she conveys the news to her husband. If embarrassed, she conveys the news to her mother-in-law or to some other female companion in the family. The happy news is conveyed to her parents by a personal visit of an old lady of the family, either her mother-in-law or her husband's elder brother's wife. The woman carries turmeric (*pasupu*), vermillion (*kumkum*) and sweets (*ariselu*) as presents to the expectant mother's natal family while communicating the news to them. In turn, her parents bring turmeric powder, vermillion, coconuts, new clothes and bangles for their daughter.

On an auspicious day, the occasion of the expectant motherhood is celebrated. She is dressed in new clothes and decorated with new bangles. The priest of the principal lineage deity (*bhaktudu*) performs a ritual in her husband's house for propitiating the lineage deities and ancestors of the family to ensure happy delivery for the expectant mother.

There are no special prescriptions or prohibitions associated with the food habits of a pregnant woman. However, the near kinsmen and relatives do entertain the expectant mother by inviting her to their houses for special dinners when she is still in her husband's house. Such invitations are mostly from her near agnates of her conjugal family and other relatives connected through her natal family.

The expectant mother attends to all types of household work in the family till the sixth month of her conception. When she attains the seventh month, the parents of the girl take the expectant mother to her natal family for the delivery.[3] It is the practice among the Jalaris that the first and second deliveries of the woman should take place in the house of her parents. However, if a woman has no parents, her elder brother invites her to his house for delivery.

The Jalaris do not go to the nearby maternity centre situated at a distance of 8 kms. at Kanithi Primary Health Centre for delivery. The village has its own midwives and depends solely on the services of the local midwives (*mantrasani*). Two old women of the village are conducting maternity services. Delivery is conducted in a house where *gondillu* is not situated. They take care to see that the *gondillu* is not polluted by birth.

The pregnant woman attends to household duties till she experiences labour pains. When labour pains start she is made to rest on a cot in the room set apart for child birth. The local midwife is immediately summoned to attend to her. The near and dear ones stay with her for necessary assistance. Before the local midwife enters this room she cleans her hands and feet with water and invokes the deities and ancestors of the family and the village for a successful delivery.

As soon as the child is born, the umbilical cord is cut with a knife which the local midwife brings with her. After separation of the child, oven ash is applied to the umbilical cord of the child. Placenta is taken out by an old woman of the family and buried in the backyard. Later, the child is given bath with hot water after applying turmeric paste to the child. Near kinsmen and relatives, including the husband and parents-in-law of the women are invited and the baby is shown to them. The child is believed to resemble its father or mother.

The mother is not allowed to go out of the house for three days, during which period the midwife attends to the mother and the child. An earthen pot containing cinder is kept below the cot for keeping the room warm. Both the mother and the child are fomented to relieve their bodily pains and keep them warm. Her diet in this period consists of a medicinal preparation known as *kayakam*. It is prepared with boiled garlic, jaggery and other herbs with oil. This is administered three times a day. The baby is put to mother's breast from the third day onwards.

Childbirth and Pollution

Childbirth creates a complex social and ritual situation characterized by varieties of notions.[4] Childbirth causes polution not only to mother and child, but also to members of her husband's family and their agnates. But if a woman gives birth in her natal household, the members of that family do not suffer pollution, except those that attend on her and such pollution disappears with a bath.

The mother and her new born child are said to be in a state of ritual pollution considered dangerous. They are considered as possible sources of ritual pollution to other persons who come into contact with them. Therefore, they are kept in seclusion for a specific period till they undergo purificatory rites to mark the end of the period of pollution and their formal incorporation into the social environment.

The period of pollution caused by childbirth ends on the ninth day and both the mother and the child are given a bath with hot water boiled with *vavili* leaves to mark their ritual purification. When a mother is reincorporated into her usual social environment, she may resume her normal relations within the household. She usually comes out of the house to attend to her household duties from the ninth day onwards.

Similarly, family members and their agnates, who are under pollution, bathe at the house of child birth for ritual purification. During this period, sacrifices to the ancestors and family deities are performed with general intent of inducing them to adopt a benevolent attitude towards the child and its mother and to protect them from all other evil spirits. A feast is arranged for agnatically related kinsmen and affines to celebrate the childbirth. The washerman takes the polluted clothes for purification and returns on the ninth day. He is suitably paid for his services.

Naming Ceremony and "Incorporation"

The transition from a state of pollution of a new born child and his incorporation into the social environment through ritual purification does not confer on the child with a membership in the family in which it is born. The social and spiritual significance of the new born child is recognised when it is ritually given a name and formally 'incorporated' into the family. Such formal incorporation of the child into the family signifies social acceptance of its father, mother and other kinsmen of the household and kinship bonds between the child and other kinsmen are ceremonially established.

Naming ceremony takes place either on the ninth or eleventh day of child-birth. The Jalaris are named after their lineage deities. Children are usually given the names of their ancestors. In Jalaripalem, the usual practice is to name the new-born child after one of its deceased paternal grand-parents. The practice is strictly observed in case of first born male child of the family. The Jalaris believe that ancestors belonging to the senior generation come back to the family as sons of their sons.

The child is given a bath of the day of the naming ceremony and kept in the house (*peddillu*) where they worship their lineage deities. All the elders of the lineage attend the ceremony. The lineage priest (*bhaktudu*) performs the ceremony and offers prayers to deities and ancestors of the family, one after the other, by name. After his prayers to deities and ancestors are over, the lineage priest goes into communion with the deities and gets instructions from a particular deity or an ancestor to have its name given to the child. He tells him that a particular deity or ancestor instructed him to give its name to the child. The head of the family then offers special prayers to that particular deity or ancestor invoking that hereafter the welfare and well-being of the child is in the hands of that particular deity. Then he takes turmeric powder and vermillion from the image of that particular deity and puts it on his forehead and on the forehead of the child: a ritual that establishes the child's identity in the cultural realm with 'code of conduct'.

ADOPTION : A SUBSTITUTE TO BIRTH

Failure to beget a child creates serious problems to a Jalari couple. Those without children adopt a child, and the choice of a particular child for adoption generally reflects their anxiety to minimize uncertainties involved in an adoption. There are only five cases of adoption reported in the village.

Adoption is resorted to when a couple has lost hopes of begetting a male child of their own, so necessary to keep the descent line of the family. When a Jalari does not beget a male child through his wife, he is allowed to marry a second wife. Generally, a man and his wife decide to adopt a male child when they realise that they cannot beget a male child of their own. So also, when a couple has all male children they would adopt a female child. There was one such case recorded in Jalaripalem.

Conflicts develop when a couple are blessed with a male child of their own after they have adopted a boy. Vadamodili Appanna adopted a male child as his wife proved sterile. Then his wife became pregnant and gave birth to two male and two female children. Thereafter, the adopted son was neglected.

Trouble started in the family when his adopted son and his natural sons grew up and Appanna became old. His eldest son, the adopted one, was entrusted with family affairs which gave him the status of head of the family. The other two natural born sons of Appanna, refused to accept his authority over the family as they were conscious of the fact that their 'elder brother' was an adopted son, and not born to their parents. This led to quarrels in the family. The adopted son with his wife left the house voluntarily to avert the rift between his younger brothers and his father. But such cases are rare. Although a man supports his adoptive parents in their old age, performs the religious ceremonies of the family, offers oblations after they are dead and continues the family line of his father, he is still considered a poor substitute for a natural son.

The most eligible person to be adopted as a son is a child of one's agnate, preferably a brother's son. The adoption of an agnate is the most approved and convenient way to please both his family and the agnates of his local descent group.[5] The willingness of a brother to give his son to another brother meets no opposition in his family since the child remains a member of his own "family" and its local lineage group to which he naturally belongs.

In one case, a kinsman of his wife was adopted by one Nolli Masenu. He adopted his wife's classificatory brother's son, belonging to the Chintapalli family, mainly on the insistence of his wife. His agnates protested against it because the child was not eligible for adoption as he belonged to the family of their immediate affines. Moreover, Masenu was old and had considerable property of his own to be inherited by his immediate agnates. His agnates, particularly his brothers, protested against his choice. They offered their own sons to him for adoption. But he ignored their protests as well as their offers and adopted the child from his affinal lineage, the Chintapalli family.

In other cases, the adoptive fathers have chosen children of their agnatic kinsmen. The adoptive fathers have considerable freedom and it is entirely their preference in the choice of a child, etc. After adoption of a child into a particular family, the natural parents of the child may visit him occasionally, but they are not allowed to come when the child grows up and can understand things.

When adoption takes place, naming ceremony is performed in the family of the adoptive father. Village elders and the natural parents of the child are invited to the ceremony and to the feast the adoptive father gives. In case the child belongs to a different caste, the adoptive father should give a feast to his fellow caste people as a mark of approval by the community for the formal incorporation of the child into his family and caste.[6] Then the naming ceremony is performed by the man's lineage priest. On that day, the adoptive father invites the priest of the village, representing all the local lineage groups as well as the village head and the heads of the local lineage groups. The adoptive father performs ceremony to the ancestors of his family and the deities of his lineage and performs the naming ceremony for the adopted child. Usually, a feast is organized the day after the adoption ceremony to the village and lineage priests and kinsmen. If the adoptive father and the natural father belong to the same local descent group no such community feasts are necessary, except the informal agreement of adoption before the heads of the village.

By giving away a child in adoption, a natural father and his family cease to have any rights over the child. Adoption means severence of all social, ritual and economic ties inherited by birth. The adopted child does not inherit the property from the natural father; and a parents' rights and obligations are transferred from the natural parents to the adoptive parents. The adopted child acquires membership of the family of its adoptive father through 'incorporation' into his family and assumes the family name of its adopted father. The adoptive father's family has rights over the child and in turn the adopted child owes ritual and moral rights and obligations towards his adoptive parents, his family and its lineage. The adopted child also participates in the social, religious and economic activities of the family and its lineage as a member of that family to which his adoptive father belongs. As already noted in the case of Nolli Masenu's adopted son, he is considered a member of Nolli family and the lineage, though he was actually born in the Chintapalli family. This expresses clearly the cultural significance of the social recognition of the adopted son through 'incorporation' and 'membership' in his adoptive family, jurally binding him to the adoptive father, his kinsmen and his ancestors with a 'code of conduct'.

FAMILY AND THE INDIVIDUAL

We have already discussed the significance of the naming ceremony whereby a natural child symbolically integrates into the cultural realm and obtains a code of conduct through the process of incorporation into the family. By performing the rites and ceremonies, a father, on behalf of his family and its ancestors, accepts his obligations to an unknown soul, physically and socially bound to its body. The basis for such an incorporation is the establishment of a bond between the father and his child as well as between the child and the family ancestors and deities of the family by which the child acquires a membership into the family with morally binding rights and obligations to each other.

The reciprocity of obligations between the family and the individual is emphasized and maintained through obligatory performance of rituals and economic responsibilities between parents and children. Parent-child relationship is believed to have a physical, moral and supernatural basis. The Jalaris believe that a child owes everything of his life to his parents as he is begotten by them. The mother-child relationship, on the other hand, is close and intense and has an emotional basis. However, the father-child relationship is the very core of the Jalari cultural life whereby, a child owes its social identity and status.

The parents are expected to do their best for the well-being of their children. The last important moral obligation of the parents is to perform the marriage of their children. On the other hand, the child believes that he owes a moral obligation to his family to look after his parents in their old age, to perform rites and rituals on their death and finally to 'integrate' them ceremonially with the ancestors of the family. Such obligatory performances between parents and child not only bind them together, but also establish a continuity between ancestors and the living members of past, present and future generations of a family.

Ritual Obligation of Parents

Rituals performed relating to the child, subsequent to the naming ceremony, are acts of gratefulness of the household to the ancestors and deities and are aimed at the welfare of the child. It is considered as a moral duty on the part of parents to provide treatment during illness by inviting the lineage priest to perform rituals.

An important ritual after the naming ceremony is the tonsure ceremony. The first hair-cut takes place both in case of male and female children after the completion of the third month and before the attainment of first year, or in some cases, in the third year. Generally, they perfrom this ceremony before the child attains its first year. An auspicious day is fixed in consultation with the local astrologer and the ceremony is held in the household of the father. However, if the parents have taken a vow they fix the venue of tonsure ceremony at a particular religious place. A popular place among the Jalaris for performing the ceremony is Simhachalam Temple, near Visakhapatnam.

When the tonsure ceremony is performed at home, the barber (*mangali*) is called on that auspicious day, fixed for the purpose. A plank is palced on the *pial* of the house or on the threshold of the household. The child's father's sister sits on the plank facing towards east with the child in her lap. A part of her saree is spread in front so that the hair removed fall in it and not on the ground. The mother's brother initiates the proceedings of the ceremony by cutting the hair first.[7] About a *seer* of rice, a *seer* of paddy and some turmeric pieces are kept in a copper vessel (*ragi muntha*) which is placed near the barber as a gift for his services in the tonsure ceremony. Agnates, affines and friends are invited on that occasion and each of them offers a copper coin to the child by taking it round the head of the child and putting it in the copper water vessel. In addition to this, agnates and affines present the child with grain and money. The child's hair is disposed of in the sea. In cases where vows are taken in the name of some deity, it is preserved and disposed of when the trip is made. The child is given a bath and dressed in new clothes after the ceremony. The child's father's sister is suitably honoured with some cash gift. The barber takes the vessel containing foodgrains. A rupee is also paid to him. The hair is removed for the second time after a month. The Jalari consider tonsure ceremony the last of the rituals performed to the ancestors in the name of his family and on behalf of the child as a ritual homage to the ancestors for protecting the child.

It is also obligatory for the parents to perform the puberty rites for the daughter on her first menstruation. The Jalaris perform puberty rites to a girl on her first menstruation to mark her transition from the sacred status of childhood to the status of adolescence. These rituals also indicate and suggest the importance given to the procreative power of the girl as well as to increase her procreative capacity. The involvement of her affines who have interests in procreative capacity is noteworthy. Generally, the Jalari girls attain puberty between 12 and 13 years. On her first menstruation the girl is secluded as she is in a state of pollution. The girl is put in a separate apartment by putting a screen on the *pial*. Her mother's brother brings a palmyra mat on which the girl is made to sit in her allocated apartment. The parents consult the local astrologer to know the auspicious or inauspicious implications of the timings at which their daughter attained puberty. If the girl is married, as is the case with a few of the Jalari girls, the news is conveyed to her husband's house by a brother or a sister.

Father's married sister is invited on that occasion to make the girl sit on the mat presented by the mother's brother. Coconut and turmeric paste are placed by the side of the girl. Women folk of the village and other kinswomen visit the girl and present her with rice, clothes and fruits. Her girl friends keep company with her but stay outside of her apartment. Visits of kinsmen continue till the pollution period lasts, i.e., for five days. On the last day, the visitors sprinkle turmeric mixed rice on the head of the girl and bless her. Visitors are offered betel leaves in return.

The girl does not move out till the end of the pollution period. Every morning she is annointed with turmeric paste to her body and oil to her hair. She is served with sweets and food all these days of pollution. The utensils used for her food are kept separate. The apartment and the utensils used by the girl are purified after her final bath. Cowdung, water and cow urine are used to purify the apartment. The saree worn by the girl during this period is given away to the washerman.

In the case of a married girl, the households related to her husband's family bring her new clothes, sweets, bananas and turmeric and vermillion. These presentations are collectively known as *sare*. They are placed either on a cot or in the girl's apartment and exhibited to the kinsfolk. Sweets and fruits are distributed among the near relatives.

If the girl attains puberty on an inauspicious day, ritual is performed to escape from the evil effects. If the girl is married, the husband and the wife do not see each other till this ceremony is over. On the fifth day, the girl takes a ritual bath to mark the end of the state of pollution and her incorporation into a new status. The lineage priest prays to deities and performs a ritual. After the ritual the wife and husband are made to stand with a cloth curtain in between them. While on the floor, oil is placed in an earthen pot, and the husband is asked to look at the image of his wife in the oil and vermillion mark is put on the forehead of the girl. Immediately after one or two days or on an auspicious day, they arrange for consummation of the marriage.

Economic Obligations of the Parents

Responsibility of rearing children rests with the parents and their natal household. The Jalari children are dearly loved by their parents. The child starts life with this great asset. Kinsmen, friends and relatives come to see the child and give possible assistance in the usual duties of feeding and nursing whenever the mother is burdened with domestic household duties. Elderly women relatives come and stay with the family and look after the welfare of the child. An elderly woman of the house takes the responsibility of regularly bathing the child on alternative days till it attains the age of three months.

The child spends several hours a day in mother's arms in its early childhood. The little child is looked after with indulgence, attentive care and cheerful patience at this stage. It lives exclusively on mother's milk for about six months. Thereafter soft cooked food is given as supplementary food and the child continues to suckle the mother's breast till it develops taste and preference for cooked food. Usually a child is breast-fed till three years of age. There are a few cases where a child is allowed breast feeding until he is five. However, a child is weaned much earlier if a younger sibling is born.

The child is always in the company of an adult or an elder sibling until it is five or six. A father spends much of his leisure time in the company of his children. In general children help or watch the work of the mother or father. Female children help the mother in the household while the male children watch and help the father in his repairs of damaged nets on his return from the sea.

Children are expected to obey the commands of the elders, particularly those of their parents.[8] The young child generally moves more closely to the mother than the father as he spends more time with the mother in the household as she attends to her domestic work. She is also responsible for teaching the child discipline in its early stages. Therefore, the child's attachment to its mother is greater in infancy. If the father beats the child when it disobeys him, the latter seeks refuge with its mother;

and if the parents beat, it seeks refuge with the grandparents. A child enjoys more freedom and care with grandparents than with parents.

From the age of five and above his father prepares a cast-net for his son to catch small fish on the shore and in the backwaters. Children are employed to look after the catch and the belongings of net group after it is drawn to the shore, for which they are rewarded with some fish as remuneration. Childhood continues till a boy reaches his twelfth year. Then he takes part in fishing activity along with the adults. After a boy gains considerable experience, he is included in one of the net groups as a member of the crew and is paid only half the share of what an adult member of the crew gets. In fact, this is a training period for the boy to develop himself into a good fisherman.

As the child grows, relative independence emerges between the parents and the child; daughters move out of the household after their marriage and sons assert their independence by contributing their labour and services to the household thereby increasing its income.

When a boy starts participating actively in fishing expeditions with the net groups, his relations outside the family are expanded and consequently assumes new status and roles in his day to day interaction. This is an important phase in the individual's life cycle and his care-free boyhood life comes to an end with marriage. The Jalari parents consider that it is their duty to perform the marriage of their children when they come of age; a moral obligation they owe to the person, ancestors and deities of the family.

Ritual Complex of Marriage Ceremony

A Series of rites involving the individuals, ancestors and deities constitute the marriage ceremony among the Jalari rituals performed in the marriage ceremony serve two purposes. First, rituals that precede marriage ritual are to intercede with the deities, ancestors and evil spirits so that their wrath may not fall on the proper ritual. Marriage ritual, on the other hand is contended to seek the blessings of the deities and ancestors and the elders and society, besides binding the man and his wife in a relationship with a code of conduct.

When both the parties agree to the marriage, the ceremony is fixed usually after the completion of the big-net fishing season. Then the boy's party consults the local astrologer to fix an auspicious day for performing the marriage ritual. A man from the groom's household is sent to the girl's house to inform the date of marriage ritual and asks them to get ready for the marriage ceremony. In the meanwhile, the head of the boy's household, with the assistance of the village functionary (*sammiti*), goes round the village inviting each and every member of the household in the village. He also goes outside his village to invite kinsmen, relatives and friends to attend the marriage ceremony.

The ceremony starts with the worship of ancestors and lineage deities early in the morning on the marriage day. Food specially cooked for the marriage feast is first offered ceremonially to the ancestors and deities. Then the boy is ceremonially prepared as a bridegroom (*pelli koduku*) through a simple ceremony to separate him from the secular world to a state of ritual purity. The boy is seated on a wooden plank facing towards east. The barber attends to the removal of his nails of his toes. This is known as *kali gollu theeyuta*. Then he is anointed with turmeric and oil by five women of married status selected specially for this purpose and given a ceremonial bath. He adorns with new clothes and gold ornaments, usually a gold chain in his neck and finger rings. A little of paddy is put in a basket and pounded with a pestle (*rokali*) by the five women of married status. Then the pestle is touched on shoulders and knees of the bridegroom. The paddy is given away to the barber for his services. Then the priest of the lineage (*bhaktudu*) administers the ceremony and ties *kankanam* on the wrist of right hand of the bridegroom to mark the ritual status of the boy as a bridegroom.

In the same way, the bride is also ceremonially prepared at her residence. After this ceremony the bride's party along with the bride starts for the bridegroom's place. If the bride belongs to another village the bride's party stops at the outskirts of the boy's village. The village functionary along with other relatives of the boy's household, receives them. Then he goes to the house of the bridegroom and informs them of the arrival of the bride and her party. The groom's party receives them with drums and trumpets and leads them into the village.

At the groom's house, ceremonial posts (*pandiri ratalu*) are erected as a marriage pandal (*pelli pandiri*) for the purpose of celebrating marriage. An earthen dais (*peenu*) is constructed in the centre and straight in front of the main entrance of the house. This dais is decorated with rice flower, turmeric powder and vermillion, representing three colours of white, yellow and red. A wooden seat (*peeta*) is kept on the dais and covered with a white cloth, a *saree* or a blanket.

Later that night, bridegroom's household arranges a marriage feast to the villagers, the bride's party and other special invitees from other villages. Every household of the village is invited to the feast. Before twelve in the night, the bridegroom takes a ride (*vuregimpu*) on a horse which is customary only to the Jalaris of this region. The groom goes through the main streets of the village to the outskirts of the village. Then he rides further and reaches the shrines of the village deities. There he climbs down from the horse and offers special prayers to the village deities. Later, he returns back to the village on horseback.

At about twelve in the night the bridegroom returns to his house with his friends and enters the marriage *pandal* for the marriage ceremony. The bridegroom is dressed for this purpose with a *dothee*, a shirt and a head-gear (*paga*). He is taken round the dais (*pelli peenu*) three times and seated on the wooden plank placed on the earthen dais, facing towards east. Likewise, the bride is brought into the pandal duly decorated with turmeric coloured sari (*pasupu koka*) and gold ornaments and seated to the left of the bridegroom. It is the custom among the Jalaris that the maternal uncle of the bride should bring the bride in a basket into the pandal. The maternal uncle (MB) receives a token gift of rupees five from the bridegroom for bringing the bride into the pandal. The lineage priest (*bhaktudu*) or the local astrologer performs the marriage ceremony. He distributes *akshintalu*, rice mixed with turmeric powder, to all persons assembled under the pandal. The marriage locket (*sathamanam* or *pusthe*) is sent round to the elders for their blessings. Belief is that the touch of the elders to the *sathamanam* sanctifies the marriage. The priest of the lineage or the local astrologer gives the *sathamanam* to the bridegroom who ties it round the neck of the bride at the auspicious time (*muhurtham*) fixed for the purpose. On that occasion, all the elders that assembled there shower *akshintalu* on the heads of newly wedded couple with their blessings. In old times the marriage ceremony used to be conducted by the priest of the local lineage group. He also used to tie the *pusthe* around the neck of the bride, not the bridegroom. Now-a-days, the local astrologer conducts the ritual and the marriage ceremony.

After the conclusion of the marriage ritual, the end of the bridegroom's *dothee* and the hem of the bride's yellow *saree* (*pasupu koka*) are knotted as to signify the wedlock of the couple. Then the newly wedded couple is taken in procession round the village. Finally, they visit *peddillu* of the bridegroom's descent group to offer prayers to the family deities. Then the couple is taken in procession through the main streets of the village to the shrines of the village deities. The newly married couple offer their prayers to the village deities under the direction of the four *dasullu* of the village. After worshipping the village deities, the couple returns to the village. Finally, they reach the house of the bridegroom. The entrance of the bride into her husband's household after the marriage ceremony is ceremonially conducted and is known as *gadapa thokkadam*.

That morning, the relatives and friends present gifts to the bride and bridegroom both in the form of cash and kind (*katnalu kanukalu*). The same evening, *kankanalu* from the wrists of the bride and bridegroom are removed to mark the end of the ritual status of the bride and the bridegroom.

The next morning the bride's party takes the girl and the boy to the bride's residence. This is known as *enalu*. The bridegroom stays at his wife's natal household for three days. At the end of the third day, the parents of the girl take the couple back to the boy's residence, along with marriage gifts and other items of *sare*, as agreed during the marriage negotiations. The *sare* usually consists of articles useful to the couple to set up a new household, such as a cot, chairs, household utensils, etc., alongwith fruits and sweets. This marks the formal handing over of the girl (*appaginthalu*) by her parents to the parents of the boy.

Consummation (*garbadhanam* or *karyam*) is performed in the household of the boy after the return of the married couple. If the girl is young and has not attained puberty, consummation is postponed. In the case of mature girls it is performed three or five days after the marriage, in consultation with the local astrologer on an auspicious day.

Marital status is an important event in the life of a fisherman for it provides him a respectable place in the society as an adult. It enables him to participate in the socio-political and religious activities of the community. Soon after marriage, his rights and obligations to the natal family take a marked change. Until this stage, a son is supported by his parents, and during his youth, parents are not much bothered what he earns and how much he gives to his parents. With marriage the situation changes. He is an adult and is expected to play an important role in his family's social, economic and religious activities as well as in the society. He is expected to earn money to support not only his parents and other dependent siblings of his family, but also his wife and his family establishment. Now he is expected to perform his duties, morally and culturally defined 'codes of conduct' binding him with his parents, siblings, ancestors and deities.

Old Age

The Jalari society places no maximum age limit for retirement. When a man is unable to do his routine economic activity, he stops going for fishing. In some cases, his sons may advise him to take rest. In general, an old man himself takes the decision when he must stop taking active part in fishing activity. However, he cannot stop doing any work and hence takes a subsidiary role in fishing activity, such as attending to repairs of nets and boats, etc.

There are twenty-four old persons in the village. The oldest man in the village is 71 years of age. Many of them lose their sight at an early age and retire from active participation in fishing. There are also a few persons in their fifties who are blind. A common disease among fishermen is loss of sight at an early age possibly due to unhygienic working and living conditions.

Old men spend most of their time on the sea-shore when boats reach the shore. When a man or woman becomes enfeebled by old age or is otherwise unable to work to earn livelihood, his/her children are expected to look after him. If old parents desire to live separately from their sons, each of their sons contribute towards their maintenance. It is said that in theory each of his sons should contribute one fourth of his individual income, however, the general pattern is that many of the old parents live with one of their sons.

Women are relatively younger than their husbands. An old woman keeps herself economically active by engaging in fish trade. As long as she is able to maintain the house and cook food for her husband, she and her husband live together in a separate household of their own.

As age creeps in, participation of the old in the household affairs shows a marked decrease. Old man's role as head of the household is slowly transferred to his eldest son, while the daughter-in-law slowly assumes the role of her mother-in-law. However, an old man's participation in religious and political activities of the family and the lineage increases with age and he is consulted during such activities. The old woman, on the other hand, continues to be active in economic affairs of the family by selling fish in the nearby markets thereby contributing to the household income.

Death and Ritual Obligations

When the fishermen know that a man is dying, he is slowly removed from the cot and placed on a mat outside the living room. Near kinsmen assemble at his side to pour drops of water in his mouth. His agnates and affines begin making the mourning group. Elderly men make preparations for the last journey of the deceased. In case the dead man has his wife alive, his head and chin are shaved. The corpse is given bath and smeared with turmeric powder and oil. In case, the deceased is a woman and her husband is alive, the husband is the first person to pour water. He applies turmeric powder and oil to the dead body and other members of the family do the same afterwards.

The floor on which the person breathed his last is cleaned and plastered with cow-dung and a wooden plank is placed on it. After the ceremonial bath the corpse is dressed with new clothes. Turmeric, vermillion and flowers are profusely used for adorning the body. An earthen oil lamp is lit beside the head of the body.

Freshly cooked rice mixed with jaggery and milk is offered in the name of the deceased in a green leaf. His eldest son takes morsel of this food to the mouth of the corpse twice.

A group of kinsmen and friends gather in front of the house to carry the body to the funeral ground. They are mostly agnates, affinal relatives, friends and fellow-caste men. A funeral bier to carry the corpse is prepared and the body is placed on the bier and tied with coir rope.

The funeral processing starts from the house accompanied by musical instruments. The procession is led by the chief mourner who is the eldest son of the deceased person. If the deceased person has no sons the chief mourner is one of the male agnates of his family or their sons.[9] The chief mourner carries flowers and paddy mixed with turmeric paste in a vessel throwing it over the corpse as other relatives follow him carrying the corpse.

On reaching the funeral ground the corpse is taken round the pyre thrice and placed down. The corpse is removed from the bier, lifted up and placed on the pyre by those who carried the corpse on the bamboo frame. If the deceased person is a male, the head is placed towards the east and if a female, the head is placed towards the west. In case of a female the face is kept downwards facing the ground and in the case of a male the body is kept facing upwards. The chief mourner lits the pyre beginning from the side where the head lies.

When the funeral fire rages upward, the chief mourner goes round the pyre thrice carrying a pot of water. At the end of each round, one of the persons who carried the corpse, strikes against the pot and makes a hole. The water comes out through the hole of the pot as he walks round the pyre. As the chief mourner completes the last round, the water pot on his shoulder is completely broken by the last stroke and he goes forward without looking back and all the participants in the procession disperse and take bath in the sea.

Death pollution lasts for eleven days in the case of adults. On the twelfth day, a purification ceremony is performed. In case of children below six years, pollution lasts up to the third or fifth day. Members belonging to the lineage of the deceased observe death pollution and all auspicious ceremonies are prohibited during this period.

In case of a married woman, her natal household and its lineage do not observe pollution but the woman's husband's family and its lineage observe pollution. However, the expenses involved in the cremation of the dead dody are borne by her brother, as a part of the affinal obligation of his family.[10] From the day of cremation till the end of the period of pollution, an oil lamp is lit at the grave of the deceased person every morning and evening. For the first three days the chief mourner visits the grave and lits the oil lamp and later it may be performed by any member of his family.

Only adults are cremated while children are usually buried. In case of children, they place milk on the grave of the deceased child, along with an oil lamp. Only in such cases where the deceased died of an epidemic or where he expressed a desire to be buried, they bury the corpse instead of cremating it. Both the practices of burial and cremation signify the transformation and termination of an individual's relationship with the world, it generates a relationship between the living and the dead.

Obsequies Ceremonies

The Jalaris believe that the dead person who is buried or cremated belongs to neither this world nor of the world of ancestors. The following rituals and ceremonies are ultimately aimed at 'mixing him with the ancestors'.

On the third day, an obsequies ceremony known as *chinadinam* is observed. Members of the household take bath. A *satani*, a non-Brahman priest, of Vaishnava sect is invited to officiate and conduct the obsequies ceremony. The chief mourner, *satani*, and those who carried the corpse to the burial ground proceed to the grave. They take with them cooked rice, curries or various types of sweets, mostly those of which the deceased was very fond of. On reaching the funeral ground the persons who accompanied the chief mourner and *satani* collect the ashes of the deceased person. Three bones are taken out and bundled in a cloth and tied to the branch of a tree. These bones are used for obsequial purposes on the final day of purification ceremony.

The ashes are divided into three equal parts. The offerings brought by the chief mourner are served in front of the three portions of the ashes in the name of the deceased. Later, some of these offerings are taken and placed in a small pit dug in the cremation ground. For some time they leave that place and watch from a distance till the offerings are touched by a crow. This is a sign, they believe, that the deceased was satisfied and has accepted the offerings of the chief mourner and his family. The remaining offerings are eaten by the persons who accompany the chief mourner and the *satani*. During these operations and offerings, the *satani* recites prayers for the deceased. At the end of the ceremony, all of them return home with the collected ashes.

Death pollution ends on the eleventh day and the final obsequies are performed on the next day. All the agnates are invited on this occasion. *Sathani* conducts the ceremony at the house of the deceased. In the evening hours a non-vegetarian food is prepared to offer in the name of the chief mourner. Afterwards, he goes to the sea-shore where he immerses the ashes of the deceased. In case, the deceased happens to be the wife of the chief mourner, he is taken by the *satani* and the other men, who carried the corpse, to the sea-shore. There he takes bath and removes his waist-thread (*molathadu*). On the other hand, if the deceased had a wife, she is accompanied by a widow to the sea-shore where her bangles and *pusthe* or *thali* (marriage locket) are removed by the latter. No male members are allowed to participate. The accompanying widow gives her bath and she is dressed in a new white saree. Thereafter, she never wears coloured clothes and is forbidden to use bangles. Her old saree is given to the washerman.

Then the chief mourner is brought home and is seated by the side of *satani* who keeps the deities symbolized in a small copper or brass idol on a thick spread of uncooked rice. A vessel filled with turmeric water is placed before the chief mourner. The relatives and kinsmen who come to meet the bereaved take a copper coin, turn round the chief mourner's head and look at his face as reflected in the water and directly drop the coin in the tumbler and see the deity. Thus, all the relatives and kinsmen meet the chief mourner. Kinsmen and relatives are entertained with a non-vegetarian dinner on that night.

After a month's time, another ceremony known as *nelavaram*, is observed. On this day, they serve vegetarian meal to the deceased in the *peddillu* of its lineage and offer a coconut in the name of the deceased. This is followed by a ceremony called as *moolaku thechuta*, by which they bring the departed soul back to home to be mixed with his ancestors (*peddullo kaluputa*) to provide the deceased with a place in the world of ancestors by bringing him into the family shrine (*gondillu*). Thereafter, on every *makara sankranthi* (in January) and on *kottamavasa* (Telugu New Year's day) the livings offer the ancestors with new clothes and a vegetarian meal and worship them on every important occasion of ceremonies performed in the household.

REFERENCES

1. All forms of groups are based upon some principle of recruitment whereby individuals are made members, that is, are made to assume the implicit rights and obligations. It is by this principle that groups maintain and renew themselves, and by this principle too, that individuals change into persons or add new roles to those they already hold (Nadel 1951 : 151).
2. Both the higher castes and the lower castes desire to have sons, though they attribute different reasons for it. For instance, Pandits of Kashmir say that "Children are the joy of life, the first of good *karma* and the blessings of gods. Sons are particularly auspicious and, therefore, greatly desired..." (Madan 1965 : 77). However, the lower castes make their case more directly and say they need them for support during old age (see Mandelbaum 1972 : 58-63).
3. It is common that before the birth of her first child a woman returns to her parents' home (see Mandelbaum 1972:88). In Hindi-speaking regions, a woman goes to her parents' home for a lengthy visit after the childbirth in her husband's household (Karve 1953: Lewis 1958:49)
4. "The new born infant arrives in a highly polluted state and must be carefully and gradually brought into a safer ritual and social condition. Physiological processes have produced the baby, but it is only after the family performs the proper ritual that the infant becomes a member of society. Society, not nature, has the decisive work in adding a new person to its number" (Mandelbaum 1972 : 120).
5. Writing about Pandits of Kashmir, Madan (1965), notes that preference in adoption is only for a child of an agnate and "if no child among a man's kin is available for adoption, or if he wants particularly to displease his own patrilineal kin, then he may choose a kinsman of his wife as his son", (1965:83).
6. This case of adoption of a child of different caste was collected among Jalaris of the neighbouring Dibbapalem village.
7. The important role of a mother's brother in the life cycle ceremonies from birth to marriage is an all India phenomenon (see Dumont 1957:36; Madan 1965: 213-15; Rivers 1907).
8. Deference to parents is seen among both higher and lower castes of India (see Mandelbaum 1972: 58-60).
9. When Kadiri Appalaswamy died without a son, his brother's son Gurrayya acted as the chief mourner.
10. The Jalaris consider this act as the last of the series of obligations one owes to his sister and to the wife-receiving household as a part of the obligations involved in an affinal alliance.

FOUR

HOUSEHOLD COMPOSITION

THE BASIC domestic unit among the Jalaris is the family. The term *kutumbam* is invariably used for family in its wider context and primarily a genealogical construct. It is also used as a polysemy and is applicable to any close knit kin group of a household to lineage. The Jalaris count their numbers and describe their family groupings in terms of household. The Jalari household is always a family unit usually consisting of an adult male, his wife and children. In some cases, it includes other kinsmen and their wives and children who are agnatically related to each other.

The term *illu* is used to designate the household referring to its activities and organisation. The household among the fishermen, besides being a residential group, is a property owning unit and a unit of consumption. Each household has separate means of production and a separate cooking place. The cooking place is private and others are allowed only with the permission of its owner. The household as a basic domestic group is the most clearly drawn unit in the village and its members are referred to as the group sharing the same hearth.[1] A common dwelling may have a number of such hearths in it and several households may live under the same roof but they function as distinct domestic units. Their separateness is clearly seen by the fact that households are not counted on the basis of the existence of houses, but on the basis of the number of hearths in the village.[2]

Each such household invariably represents itself as a distinct property owning group. However, the boats, nets and other valuable items of movable property are owned by the entire household but not by individual members of the household. Property is managed by the senior member of the household and the right to dispose of such property is vested in the head of the household. Earnings of different members of the household are used for its maintenance and development. However, at the time of division of the household, property is divided equally among the male members of the household who are coparceners and their rights to property are recognized.

There are 93 houses in the village as against 77 households recorded. This shows that some households in the village possess more than one house. This does not mean, however, that each house is occupied by only one household. There is, in fact, one or more households having more than one house of their own. The existence of more houses than the total number of households in the village is due to the fact that the members of many of the households dwell in more than one house. In addition to this, the various lineages have their *peddillu* in separate houses.[3]

PHYSICAL FEATURES OF THE HOUSE

The Fishermen live in thatched houses which give an appearance of hutments. There are two types of houses, locally known as *gudisillu* and *vasillu*. The *gudisillu* is constructed with its roof in an umbrella shape, supported by a central pole and resting on the circular side walls and piles as the roof slopes down. The *vasillu* is rectangular in its ground construction. Both types of houses take the name *middillu* when the ceiling of the roof is six feet above the ground level and it has a slab thickly reinforced with wood and mud and plastered with cow-dung and mud. The mud slab is covered with palmyra leaves. The thatched roof is common both for the mud plastered *middillu* and the ordinary *vasillu* and *gudisillu*. *Middillu* is preferred by fishermen for protection from fire accidents. The construction of *middillu* being expensive and laborious, there are very few such houses in the village which only the well-to-do families can afford.

Of the 93 houses of the village, only four are *vasillu* type houses and the remaining are *gudisillu* type houses. A *vasillu* is constructed either as an independent and separate structure for two or more households. The independent apartment belonging to each household is separated by a mud wall in-between them. All four *vasillu* type houses in the village belong to joint families and seem to be the most favoured type of house for them. The *gudisillu* is an independent and separate structure for each household and sometimes it is also partitioned into twc. A majority of the households live in single room houses.

The Jalaris preference for *gudisillu* type of house is well suited to the needs of an independent household (see Fig. 4.1). One roomed house with a living room-cum-kitchen (*ainillu*) is typically suited for a nuclear family, i.e., husband, wife and their offsprings. As a matter of fringe adjustment, the nuclear family may include a widowed mother

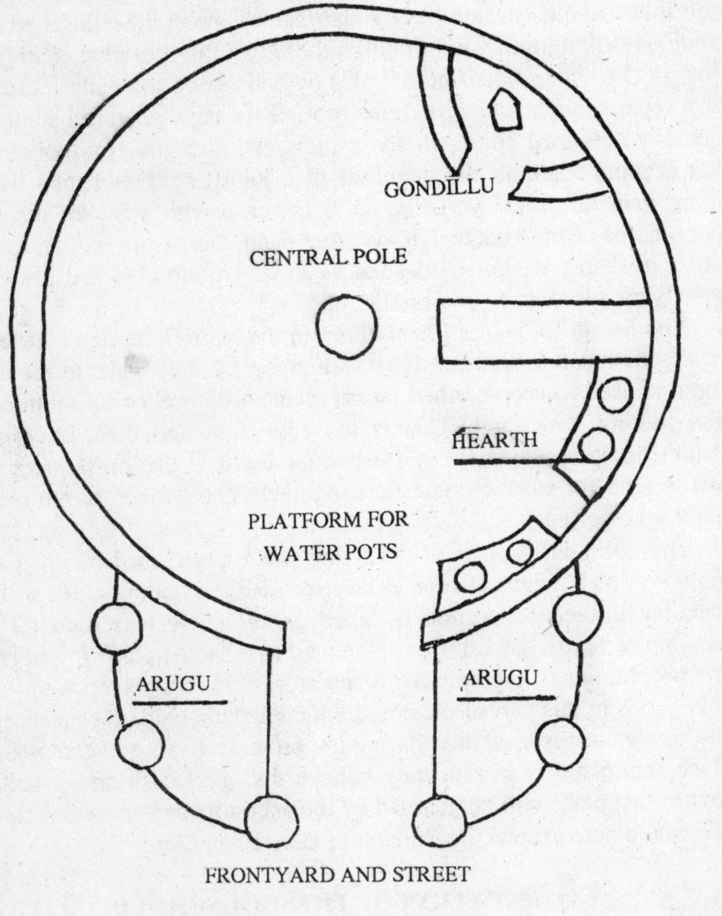

Fig. 4.1 : *Jalari Dwelling (Ground Plan of Gudisillu)*

or father, and unmarried brothers or sisters resulting into an extended family. When the family composition crosses through an extended family type, the one roomed house emerges as a full-fledged two or more roomed house to accommodate and satisfy the needs of the family generated through its internal development. This practically satisfies the needs of all the requirements of a nuclear family as well as an extended family. In course of time, if the extended family divides itself into two nuclear families by marriage of one of the unmarried male adults, resulting into a joint family, these two families may continue to live in two independent households by converting the main room into two separate units under the same roof; or the newly married adult may construct his own house. In some cases, the *gudisillu* type house may not accommodate all the members of a joint family and they live in more than one such *gudisillu*, as is the case with many of the joint households of the village. On the other hand, the *vasillu* though rectangular in shape, is similar to *gondillu* in its ground plan and preferred mostly by joint family households.

The hearth (*poyyi*) is found either in the main room or on the edge of the verandah (*arugu*). A portion aligning the side walls in the main room is used to keep earthen jars permanently installed by reinforcing and pasting with mud. This is to keep grain and other necesities. Another common element in a fisherman house is the loft (*atuku*). The loft is used for storing domestic equipment, nets broken furniture and other accessories.

The north-east corner of the living room is screened off by a thin mud-wall of a height of four to five feet and a length of three to four feet. Such screened portion is called *gondillu* which is used for the worship of family ancestors. It is treated as a sacred place for worship and propitiation of the household ancestors only. They keep their valuable goods in this part of the house which include gold, jewellery, cash and costly clothes used only during important festivals and ceremonies. Since this place is sacred, they believe that gold cash and jewellery kept in that place will be guarded by the ancestors and consequently no one would dare to steal the valuables place in *gondillu*.

COMPOSITION OF THE HOUSEHOLD

The Jalari household is a small patrilineal kin group of narrow range. It always consists of a family unit, i.e., agnatically related kinsmen, their wives and children. Rarely does the household include other kinsmen, such as sister's children and wife's siblings, etc. The female members are usually the spouses of the male agnates of the household. On marriage, a woman is brought into her father-in law's household and the process of extension, in normal conditions, continues after the marriage of other sons of the household. In the event of death of the senior man, the tendency of the married brother is to ask for a division of the household and its property.

The usual mode of post-marital residence is patrilocal and the exclusive rights of ownership to the property of the household is recognized only to the male agnates of the household. So when extension takes place, it is almost invariably in the agnatic line. The rule of patrilocal residence is strictly observed and only in exceptional cases does a man move into his wife's residence. There is only one such case where a young man, after his marriage moved into his affinal relative's house (See Fig. 4.2).

The reasons stated for this exceptional case are that this young man was brought up in the house of his maternal grandparents who lived separate from their only married son. The young man is living in the house of his grandmother (MM) along with his wife. This is an exception to the general patrilocal residence pattern. Residence of a married man in a house of his wife's relatives is not expected among the fishermen as patrilocal residence is the cultural rule.[4]

There is a considerable range in the numerical size of households (see Table 4.1) which reflects the range of variation in genealogical composition. The two households consisting of one person each are completely lacking in genealogical ramification. One is that of a middle-aged man whose wife and children died a few years ago and the other one is that of an old woman. The man lives in his house alone and prepares his own food. He often gets help from his kinsmen in the preparation of food and has close contacts with his deceased wife's family. The woman, a widow, could not stay with her son due to frequent quarrels with her daughter-in-law. As such she is living separately. The remaining households consisting of two or three generations are genealogically more complex.

The range in numerical size reflects the variation in the genealogical composition of the households in Jalaripalem. In the 77 households studied, 38 or nearly half of the households, in the village, are found to be having simple family structures. This excludes the two incomplete households and the two other households without adult male members. When such an elementary family unit with a simple genealogical composition lives independent of its natal household, it is known among the Jalaris as *vere vundadam* (separate living), as against *kalisi vundadam* (joint living), a native classification of the household composition.

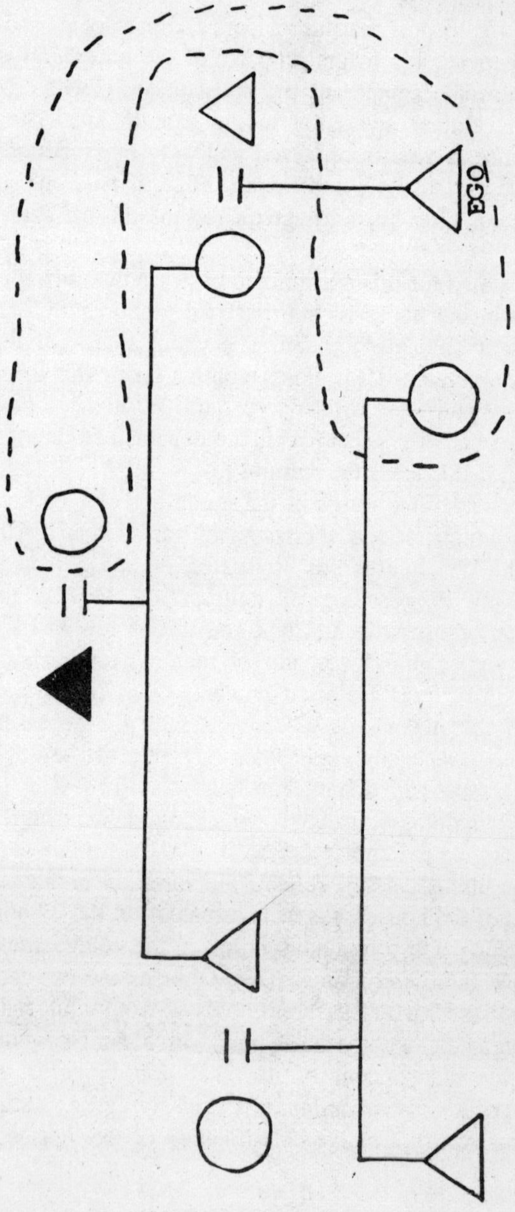

FIG. 4.2 : *An Example of Non-patrilocal Residence*

Table 4.1: Numerical Distribution of Households in Jalaripalem

No. of persons per household	*Frequency*	*Totals*
1	2	2
2	10	20
3	9	27
4	14	56
5	10	50
6	15	90
7	10	70
8	3	24
9	2	18
10	0	0
11	1	11
12	1	12
Total	77	380

The basic features of nuclear family household is the existence of a principal earning member in the household who supports other members, i.e., his wife and children, and consequently holds authority over his proteges. The husband-wife relationship is the basic bond and the determining factor, along with parent-child relationship. Such a system entitles the adult male with considerable freedom to exercise his choice in his transactions and relations with others in the world of necessity to promote the interests of his household.

Development takes place by the inclusion of the dependent agnates and the other nuclear families into the household as indicated by the remaining 35 households in the village. These households are futher classified into extended households and joint households for analytical purposes.[5] Thus extension takes place both in the nuclear family and the joint family. In the former, inclusion of dependent, such as widowed parent or unmarried siblings or both, takes place to one's nuclear family. Inclusion of unmarried brothers and sisters into one's nuclear family occurs only when one or both the parents of the children are dead. The tendency among the old widowed parents with married sons, having separate households of their own, is to live with one of them. In some cases, it was found that older parents of married children preferred to live separately in a household of their own so long they can maintain themselves.

A joint household, on the other hand, is a corporate familial group consisting of two or more nuclear families which sometimes may even include widowed parents and other unmarried siblings. Such a joint household includes two or more married brothers with their wives, children, parents and unmarried siblings. Thus, a characteristic feature of a joint household is the existence of more than one nuclear family in which the interests of the adult members conflict with each other. Yet they sink their differences, if any, as long as they live together because their personal interests coincide with the interests of the joint household. So long there is no distinction between the income and outgo of funds and so long the whole household is organized by a certain head, the persons living under these arrangements belong to a joint household. All the brothers have equal rights over the property of the household and the sons inherit father's property. Taking into consideration these characteristics and the development of genealogical composition of the households in Jalaripalem village, Table 4.2 shows classification made.

This etic classification of households composition in the village (Table 4.2) should not be construed as "exhibiting different phases of the family developmental cycle in the domestic groups in a lineal order" (Fortes, 1958: Madan 1965).[6] The classification (Table 4.2) has been made to specify the genealogical variation in the composition of the households for an analytical understanding of the process of household development. The nuclear household exhibits simple kinship structures in its genealogical composition, while the extended households exhibit further ramifications in their genealogical composition and hence complex kinship structures of two or more generations in the households.

Table 4.2 Classification of Family Structures in Jalaripalem

Type of Family	*No. of Households*	*Per cent*
Simple family structures	42	54.54
Extended family structures	17	22.08
Joint family structures	18	23.38
Total	77	100.00

The history and genealogies of the households in the village show that not all the families have passed through the various phases of the developmental cycle in the domestic groups from a simple nuclear household to extended and joint households. Major events such as birth, marriage and death do not necessarily correspond to the lineal development of the domestic groups, but they define alternate courses of social action. Some households are fitted into the pattern described by the developmental cycle in the domestic groups and some do not correlate. What is striking is that the households grow and dissolve immaturely without culminating into a joint household when the parents are still alive. Some do not dissolve even after the disappearance of its senior members and they persist as joint households in time. So the obvious explanation for such patterns of differential occurrences must be the result of processes under specific circumstances.

Therefore, the kind of explanation attempted here aims at understanding the behaviour of the Jalaris affecting the household composition as an aggregate of individual decisions. The focus of analysis is on "the determinants of choice which reflect the constraints and incentives under which people act" (Barth, 1966). In other words, the differential occurrence of genealogical pattern in the household composition reflects the Jalari's different resources, his efforts to maximise values in an arena of culturally defined constraints, incentives and the process whereby the varieties of actions and patterns are generated.

COMPOSITION OF NUCLEAR HOUSEHOLDS

The Preponderance of simple kinship structures reflects the tendency of the households to split in each generation into simple and nuclear households. There are 38 such households classified under the nuclear family grouping, forming 49.35 per cent of the total 77 households recorded in the village. This excludes the four incomplete households which are formed under exceptional circumstances by the disruption of the nuclear families. These include two one-member households and two incomplete nuclear families without an adult male member, consisting of a widow and her children.

The nuclear households include nine households with two members each composed of a wife and a husband. However, all of these households are not the establishments of recently married couples. Three of them are of old people living separately in their own households, while their sons are living separately with their wives and children. Such households will not grow in time and they disappear in the course of time. They have seen the growth and development of their households and also their premature dissolution when the married sons established their own households soon after their marriages. If one of the old couple dies, the other may join the household of one of the sons, depending upon the circumstances and alternatives open to them.

The remaining 29 nuclear households are of families consisting of an adult individual, his wife and children. The genealogical composition in these households represents two generations. The range of the numerical composition varies from three persons to a maximum of seven persons. All these households are established by the Jalari young men, either immediately after their marriage or after living with their parents for some time. Nearly 12 of these households are established by the adult males immediately after their marriage and others after living for some time with parents or married brothers. Table 4.3 shows details of genealogical composition of the households classified as nuclear households.

Table 4.3 Genealogical Composition of Simple Family Structures

Type of Household composition	*No. of generations*	*Range of kinship relations in the family group*	*Frequency*
Single membeı households	One	Widower/Widow	2
Two member households	One	Wife and husband	9
Special cases	Two	Widow and Children	2
Nuclear families	Two	Husband, wife and children	29
Total			42

The formation of nuclear households in the village appears to be affected by continual process of segmentation of the household in every generation. Division of a household property may be temporarily postponed, thus making the genealogical composition of such households more complex. However, marriage among the Jalari is an event that creates alternatives to the married male to choose between staying in his natal household or establishing a new household of his own. It is quite common among the Jalaris that initially a married adult male chooses to stay with his natal household. Only after living in his parental household with his wife for sometime or until he begets a child, he finally chooses to go separate if he believes that such an act is advantageous to promote exclusively his private assets and interests.

It is observed that married sons of the households without property, i.e., those working as sharecroppers, generally choose to separate from their natal households. Those with considerable property attached to their natal households, especially those organizing net-groups and owners of these net-groups, prefer to remain in their natal households.[7] Where property attached to household is little, the responsibilities and obligations of the elder brother are greater than the personal prestige he gains as the head of the household, the tendency seems to be to separate from the natal household soon after he gets married.

The case of Modu Appanna presented below explains some of these processes. Modu Appanna set up his own household soon after he got married. Before marriage he was living with his parents and two younger brothers and three sisters (Fig. 4.3). His father had no property, that is, nets and boats of his own and fishing was done with the net-group of his neighbour who owns them. He and his father were the only earning members. His mother had to sell fish in the markets. The income of the household was just sufficient to maintain the family. One of his mother's brothers had agreed to give his daughter in marriage to Appanna. But Appanna waited till two of his sisters got married and one of his two brothers became an earning member. His mother's brother, whose daughter was betrothed to him, also promised financial help to set up his own household. Later, he and his father borrowed Rs. 500 for his marriage. After the marriage, he asked for separation from his parents and brother. What he had inherited was a debt of Rs. 250 as his share. He moved out to one of the unused houses of his relations and set up his own household. Now, he has built his own house and is living with his wife and two children. But this does not mean that his kinsmen did not question his behaviour. Some called it an act of irresponsible behaviour but none questioned his right to separate from his natal household.

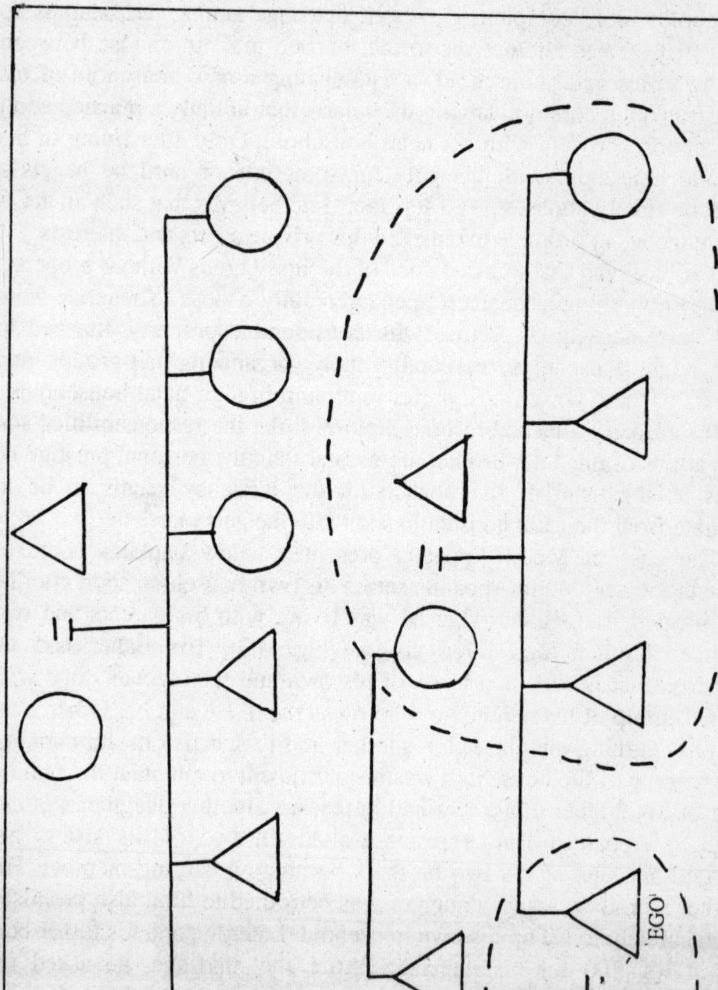

FIG. 4.3 : *Division of Household on Marriage*

However, his separation from his natal household does not deter him from participating in the day-to-day activities of his natal family. His separation from his natal household specifies his formal division of the hearth and property and he ceases to have any further claims on the property of his father and his brothers.

The most widely accepted factor for a division of the household among the Jalaris is the quarrels between mother-in-law and daughter-in-law in the household.[8] Many of the married individuals state it as the main reason for their separation. The factors that are at work in such a situation are the decision of the married men and the ever-growing interests in their respective conjugal families. The case of Nolli Bhooloka (Fig. 4.4) illustrates these points further.

Bhooloka's household consists of six members, including his wife and four children. He married when he was in his teens. He was then living with his parents and unmarried younger brother and two sisters when his wife came to live with him. Since his mother goes to the nearby *shandies* to sell fresh fish, his wife was burdened with household work of the family. There were also frequent quarrels between the daughter-in-law and the mother-in-law. His wife used to complain every night that she was burdened with the household work especially cooking and fetching water. She also used to tell and describe the harsh treatment meted out to her by the other members of the household. However, he could not take the decision to separate from his parents as he thought that it was unfair to leave his parents and the unmarried brothers and sisters after attaining adulthood which meant leaving them in a helpless condition. After some days, there was a quarrel between his wife and his mother as usual. Then he told his parents that he wanted to separate because of the quarrels in the household. He separated from his parents and subsequently set up his household. After a week's time partition of the property took place. Now his parents live with his younger brother and his wife.

This case shows that quarrels between the women of the households are not uncommon and it is the growing interests of conjugal families of the adult males in the household which make them go separate. Therefore, the motivations of the married adults to establish the household of their own are not the same in every case, but they are centred in the ever growing interests of their respective conjugal families.

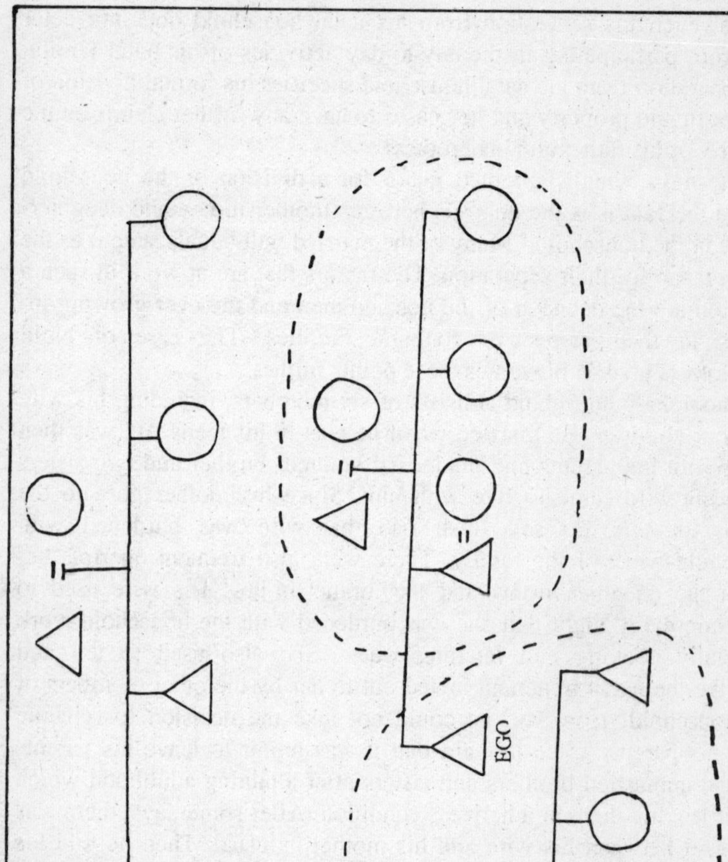

FIG. 4.4 : *Division of Household of Nolli Bhooloka*

EXTENDED HOUSEHOLDS

Inclusion of widowed parent and unmarried siblings into one's nuclear family exhibits complex genealogical composition of the household units. There are 17 such extended households in the village and in all these cases dependent widowed parent and unmarried brothers and sisters are included into one's nuclear household when disruption took place in one's natal family due to the death of one of the parents. This is part of the 'codes of conduct' an individual has to follow. Therefore, it is culturally expected of a Jalari to include his living parent and the unmarried siblings of his natal household into his household when such a disruption takes place. Further, such an act is also considered a moral obligation the Jalari owes not only to his parents and siblings, but to his family and his ancestors in general. The widowed parent in such a situation has an option either to live alone or to join the household of one of the married sons. However, the tendency in conformity with the cultural expectation among the Jalari widowed parent, is to join one of the nuclear households of their married sons.

The genealogical development of the extended households in Jalaripalem (Table 4.4) shows a marked variation in the household composition and exhibits several processes in the formation of such families.

Table 4.4: Genealogical Composition of Extended Nuclear Families

Type of Household composition	*No. of generations*	*Range of agnates included in the nuclear family*	*Frequency*
Paternal extended family	Two	Widowed parent	4
Lineal Extended Family	Three	Widowed parent and Unmarried siblings	7
Fraternal Extended families	Two	Unmarried siblings	5
Special case	Three	Mother's mother	1
Total			17

In four cases of extended households, the inclusion of an additional member to one's nuclear family took place in parental line when a widowed parent joined a son's nuclear household at the death of the other spouse. There are several processes on this pattern. For example, Kadiri Jogamma was living with her household in a household separate from those of her married sons after the formal division of their joint household. When her husband dies, she eventually joined her youngest son's nuclear household. In this case, the formation of an extended household was caused through the amalgamation of an incomplete nuclear household with that of a son's nuclear household (see Fig. 4.5).

In other cases, a joint household consisting of parents and their sons with their wives and children seem to have reduced to a paternal extended household at the death of one of the parents. For example, Nolli Bandamma and her husband were living with their youngest son and his wife and children after the formal separation of their sons. On Bandamma's husband's death, their joint household was reduced to an extended household and Bandamma continued to live with her son's nuclear family as a dependent member of the household (Fig. 4.6).

In seven other cases, the formation of the lineal extended household was caused by the inclusion of widowed parent and the unmarried siblings. This may take place under two different conditions, either through an amalgamation of a nuclear family and an incomplete family or by the disruption of a paternal or patrilineal joint household, in the event of death of one of its senior members. Kantumuchu Kunchamma, her husband and their unmarried children were living separate from her other married sons when her husband died suddenly. Then she chose to live with one of her married son's nuclear family, along with her children thus making her son's household genealogically complex (Fig. 4.7).

The other condition arises when a lineal joint household, consisting of parents, their only married son and other unmarried children, experiences death of one of the parents, thereby reducing the household to lineal extended household.

The third variation arises when the surviving widowed parent dies leaving unmarried children in the custody of one of her sons' nuclear family, resulting in fraternal extended household. There are five such households where dependent unmarried siblings are included to one's nuclear family. Such a genealogical pattern arises as a development of disruption to a lineal extended household. Kasarapu Ellamma joined her son's nuclear family along with her unmarried children when her husband died. When Ellamma also died, her son took the responsibility

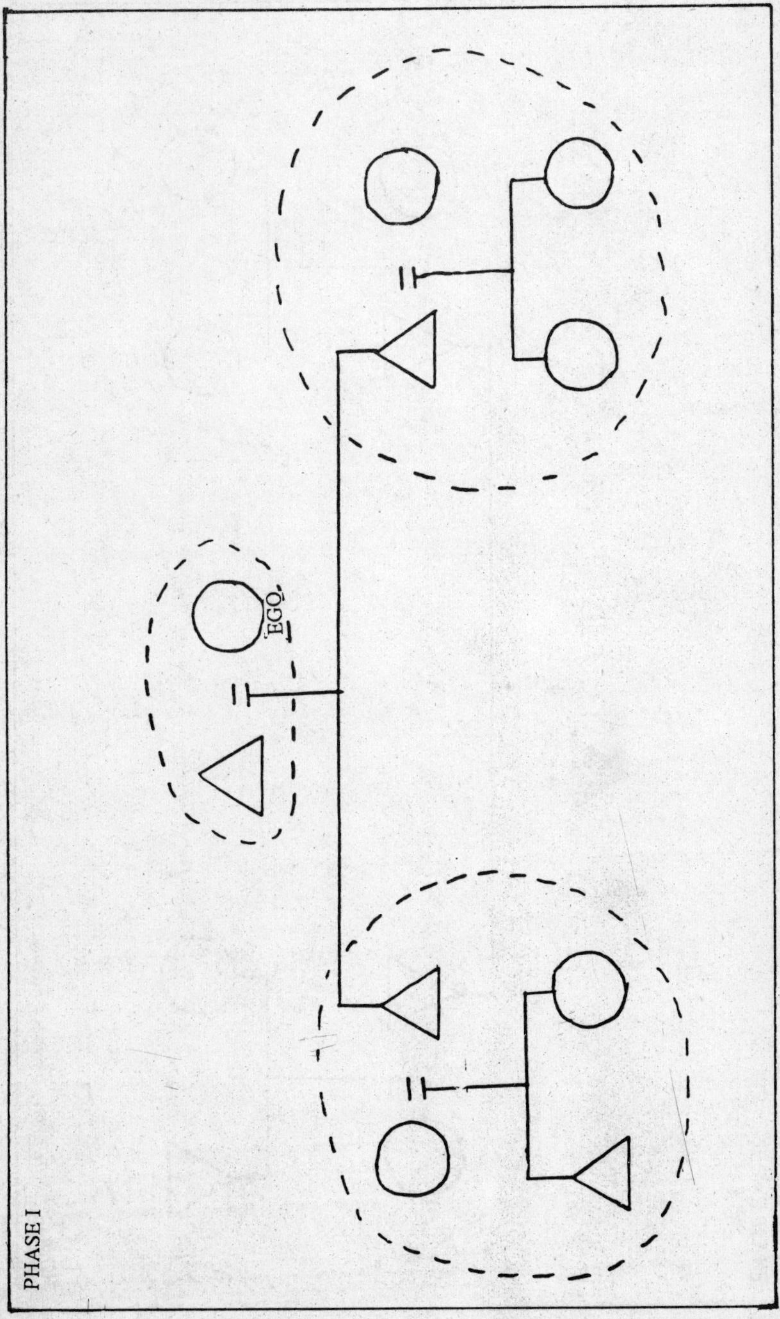
EGO
PHASE I

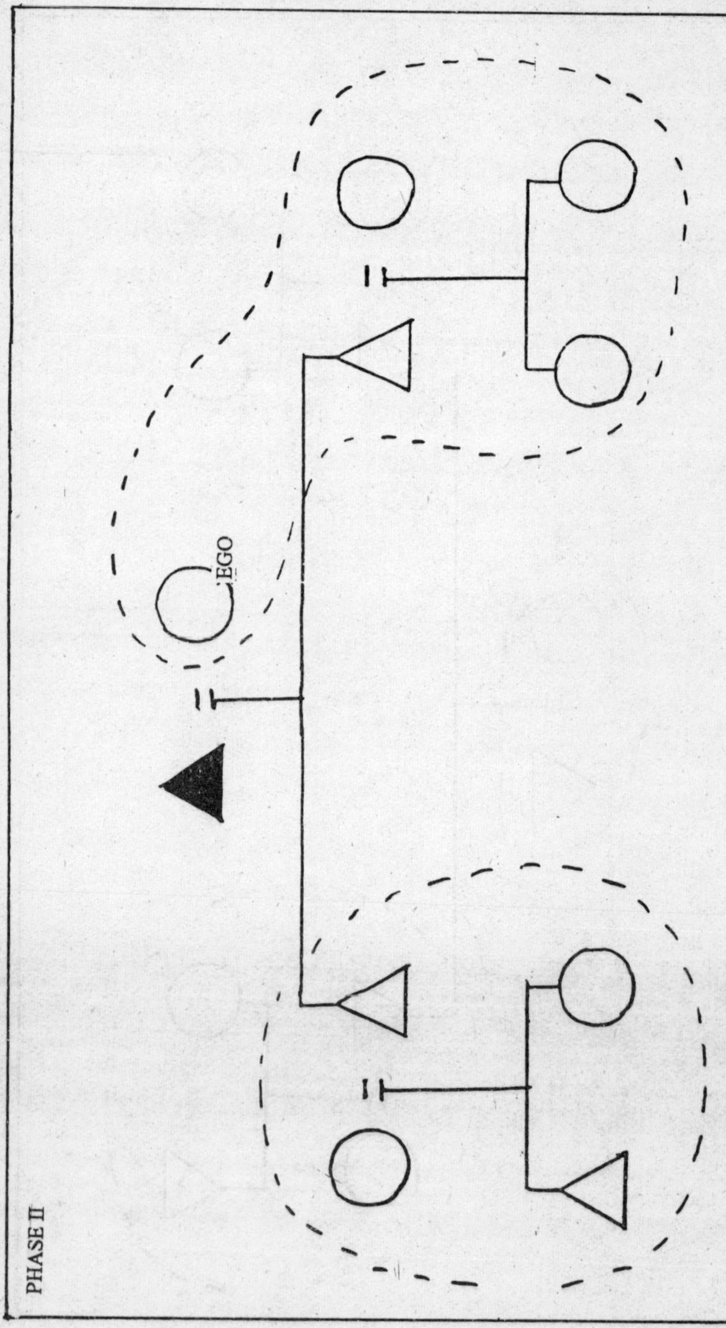

FIG. 4.5 : *Formation of Extended Family*

PHASE I

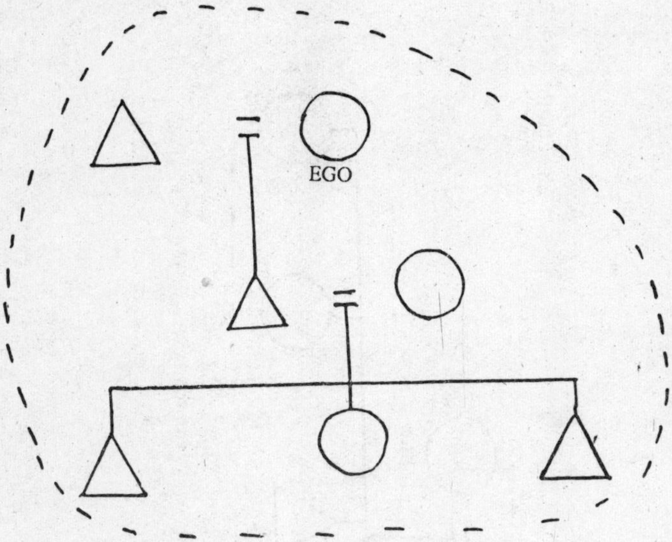

PHASE II

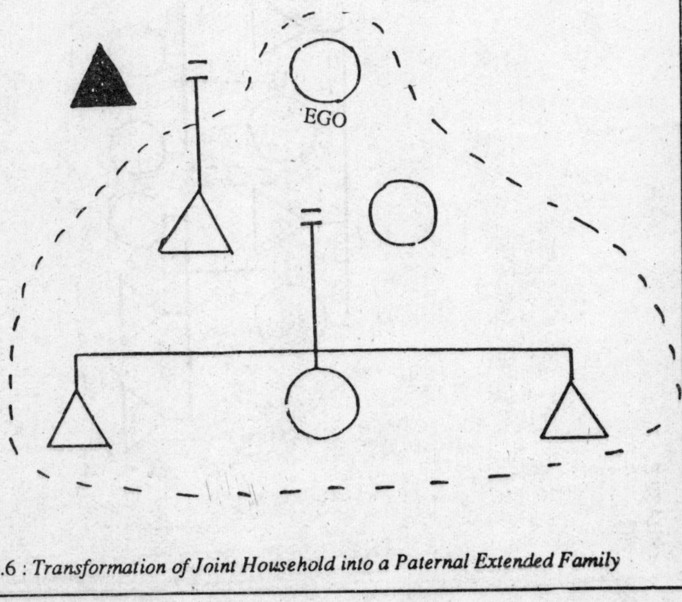

FIG. 4.6 : *Transformation of Joint Household into a Paternal Extended Family*

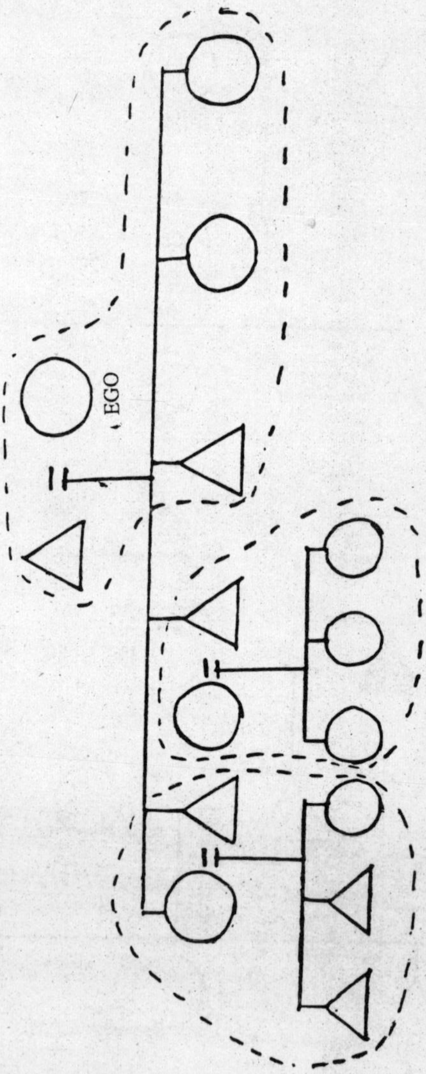

PHASE I

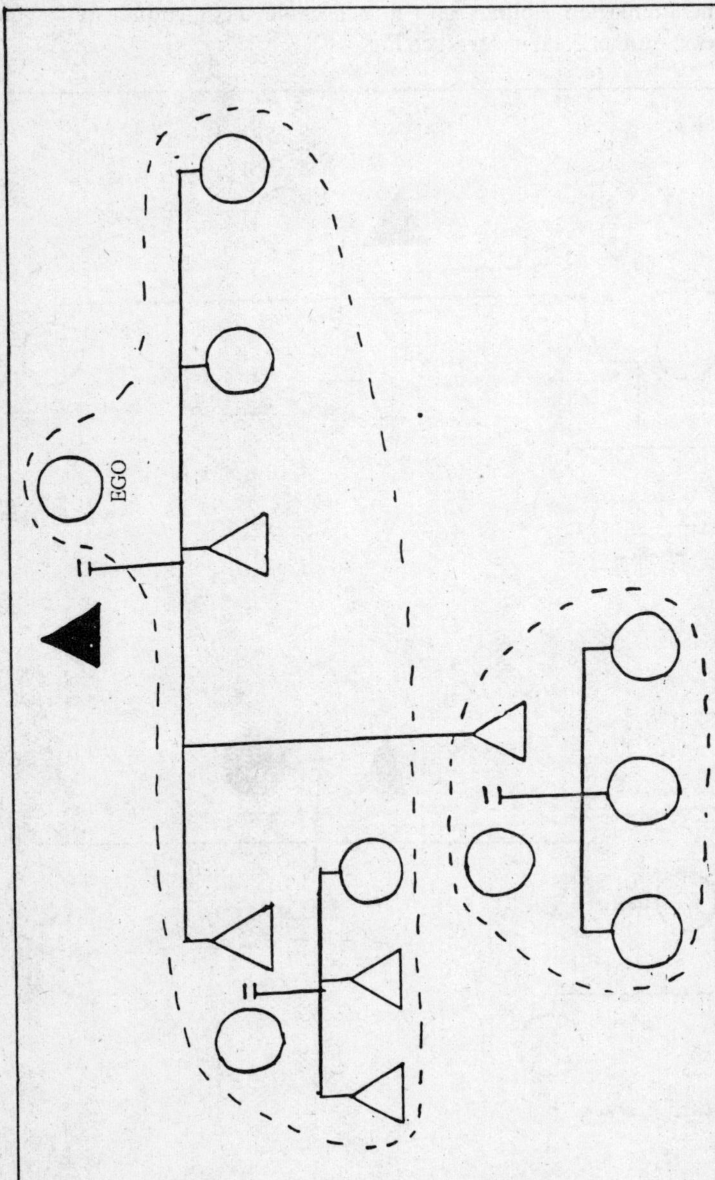

FIG 4.7 : *Amalgamation of a Nuclear Family and an incomplete Family into a Lineal Extended Family*

of the unmarried siblings and thus became the guardian to his unmarried brothers and sisters (see Fig. 4.8).

PHASE I

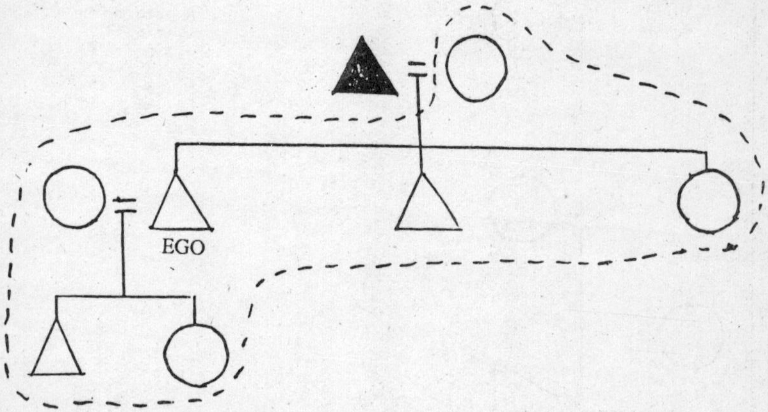

PHASE II

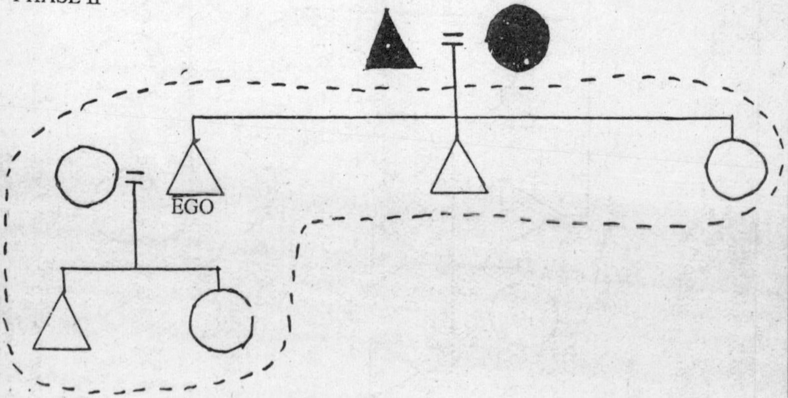

FIG. 4.8 : *Amalgamation of a Nuclear Family and an Incomplete Family into a Fraternal Extended Family*

The fourth variation in the genealogical composition of the extended family is characterised by a special case where a mother's mother was included to one's nuclear family. This is an exceptional case to the general pattern of the genealogical composition of the households in the village. The specific circumstances under which it was formed were noted earlier (Fig. 4.5).

The main contributor to the household income in an extended household is the adult son or the elder brother of the household. The aged father/mother may also help him by assisting in fishing or by selling fish in the nearby markets. Similarly, unmarried brothers/sisters also contribute to the household economy. In cases where no son/brother is willing to take the widowed parent and dependent siblings to live with him, the widowed parent and children may live in a separate household but the married and separated sons are expected to contribute towards maintenance of the widowed parent and the unmarried siblings. However, there is always one of the sons willing to take the widowed parent and his dependent siblings to live with him. But it is left to the widowed parent to choose whether to live with a son's nuclear family or not.

The situation is different when a household consisting of parents and their young children, loses one of the parents. There are two such households consisting of a widowed mother and her young children. The general pattern is that when one of the spouses is dead, the other is expected to remarry. If there are grown-up children, the widow or widower does not take normally such a step. When both the parents are dead, leaving the young children helpless, the responsibility of bringing them up rests with the married sons of the deceased parents. When children do not have adult brothers, they are taken into the household of father's brother or other agnatically related cousins of their father in the absence of a father's brother.

JOINT HOUSEHOLDS

There are 18 joint households recorded in Jalaripalem, forming 23.38 per cent of the total households in the village. Numerical strength of such households varies from six persons to twelve persons per household. The genealogical composition represents three generations in most of the cases in which two or more nuclear families live together as separate and independent household. Factors responsible for maintaining the joint family household as an independent unit are economic interests vested in the household property to which the interests of the constituent nuclear families are closely identified. The joint households are more prosperous than the other types of households so far discussed. Most of them have property rights over big-nets and have separate net-groups of their own with exclusive rights of ownership on nets and boats of the net-groups. The variation in the genealogical composition of the joint households in the village is shown in Table 4.5.

Table 4.5: Genealogical Composition of Joint Families

Type of household composition	*No. of generations*	*Range of agnates included to an elementary family*	*Frequency*
Paternal joint families	Three	Elementary families of married sons with their wives and children and unmarried children	9
Fraternal joint families	Two	Married brothers with wives and children	3
Lineal joint families	Three	Widowed parent, married brothers and with/or without unmarried siblings	5
Collateral joint families	Three	Cousins, uncles and others	1
Total			18

This categorical classification of joint households is made on the basis of the genealogical relationships between the constituent members of a joint household.[9] Every joint household in the village invariably includes parents, their sons, their wives and children, or the nuclear families of married brothers and dependents, resulting into large kin group of two or more nuclear families with complex kinship structures.

There are nine paternal joint households in the village which have grown and developed from nuclear family of an individual to a joint household when his adult sons married and decided to live together with the father's nuclear family. Such a joint household is oriented towards the dominance of the nuclear family of parents in alliance with the nuclear families of their sons. Differences and conflicts, if any, between brothers living in a joint household are minimized through the dominance of the parents and each partner finds advantages in joint action under the control of their father. This family group, however, tends to disintegrate after the death of the father.

There are three different patterns of such paternal joint households observed in the village with implications to their family organization. In two cases, the paternal joint households consists of parents with their only son with his wife and children. In such a genealogical composition, uncertainties and disintegration regarding the household's continuation are none as the interests of both the father and his son were found to be identical. If a son has differences with his father or if his wife is not on good terms with his mother, he compromises whatever differences he may have, as his father unlike a brother is not a competitor for the household property and its resources.

The other pattern of genealogical composition of paternal joint households obtains when the household consists of parents and their married sons with wives and children. There are three such households in the village which have developed from a nuclear family of the parents to the joint household on the event of marriage of their grown up sons. For example, Kadiri Kittatha and his wife are living together with three of their married sons, their wives and children. In 1963, he performed the marriage of his eldest son, Pentayya. On his marriage, Pentayya did not separate from his parents and unmarried siblings, but chose to live with his natal household. His two other sons also followed the example of their elder brother and decided to stay with their natal household after their marriage (Fig. 4.9). The maintenance of such a joint household can be achieved only through the reaffirmation of decisions on the part of the married sons who are partners in the joint household.

PHASE I

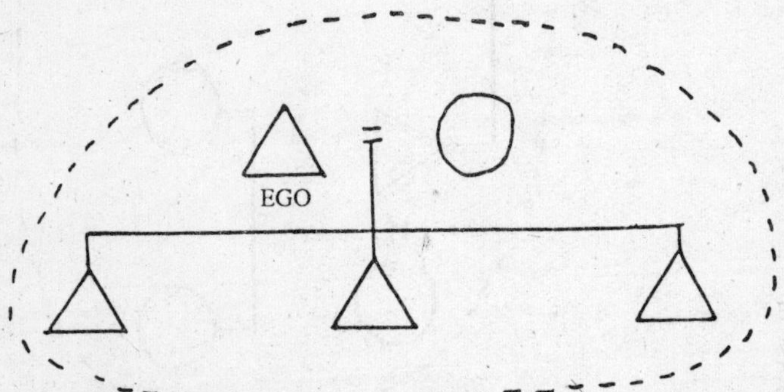

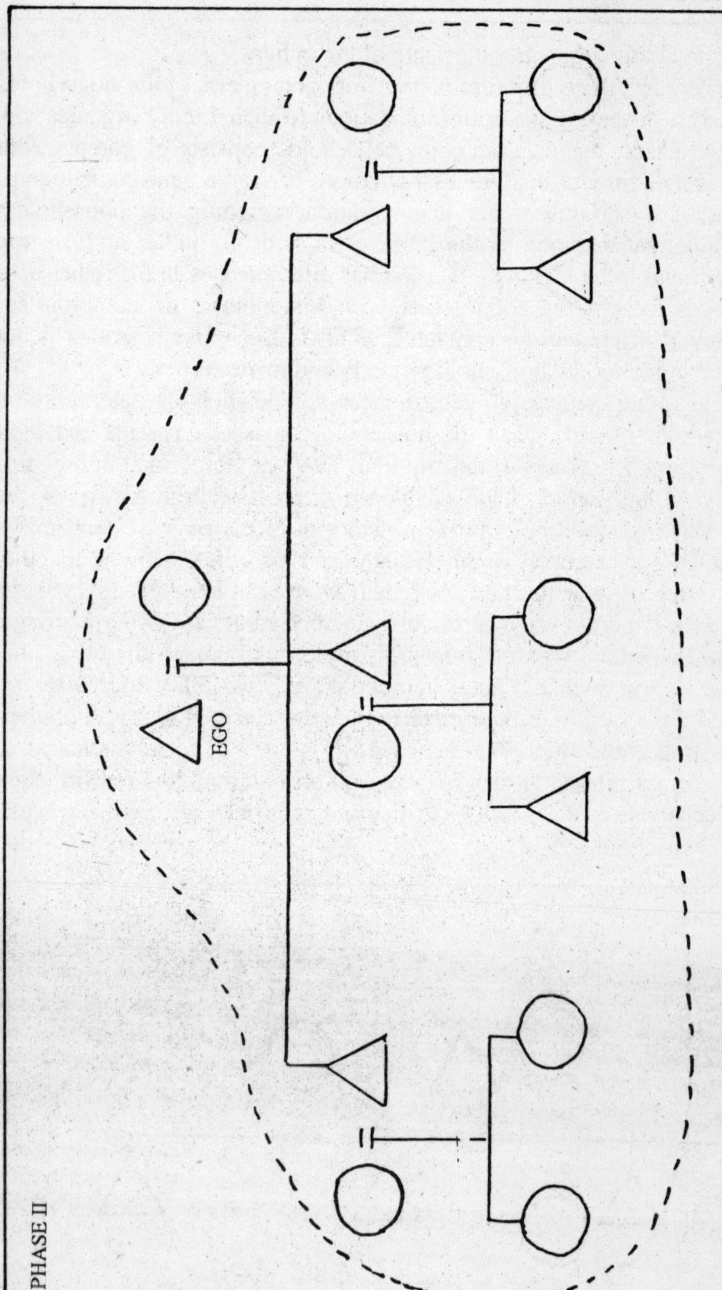

FIG. 4.9 : *Composition of a Paternal Joint Household*

The third variation of paternal joint household consists of a nuclear family of the parents with their unmarried children and married sons, their wives and children. There are four such households in the village. For example, Kantumuchu Ramaswami is living with his wife, his three sons and one daughter. His eldest son Appanna is married and decided to live with his parents in his natal household. The other two sons are still young and not married. His daughter is unmarried and living with them (fig. 4.10).

There are only three cases of fraternal joint households recorded in the village. Such a household consists of the nuclear families of two or more of brothers living together with their wives and children which they find as the most advantageous adjustment to maximize their interests. Thus the fraternal joint household depends on the warm relationships between married male siblings. The eldest of them technically stands as the head of the household who directs the activities of the household and acts as the benefactor to the rest. The alliance between the constituent nuclear families of the brothers is symbolic where all brothers hold equal rights and depend on the voluntary co-operation between potentially independent households. Such joint household continues as long as the relationship between them remains mutually satisfactory and advantageous which reflects the reaffirmation of decisions of the brothers to live together.

The component nuclear families in a fraternal joint household themselves are segments, ordered and articulated in conformity with the common interests and rules related to the joint household organization. Such a joint household is a transitory unit as its situation and circumstances continuously change in time. It splits in time into separate units when the interests of the constituent segments differ from each other. Two of the three fraternal joint households in the village belong to Kadiri lineage. These joint households have neither separated nor divided the property, which is mostly in the form of bignet shares, even after the death of the senior members.

There are five lineal joint households in the village. The existence of these joint households reflects the disruption of paternal joint households at the death of one of the parents. Three of them are joint households consisting of married brothers, their wives and children with a dependent widowed parent. The presence of a widowed parent in the joint household, undoubtedly, exerts some influence in the household functioning and also acts as a unifying factor to keep all the brothers together. The other two lineal joint households consist of

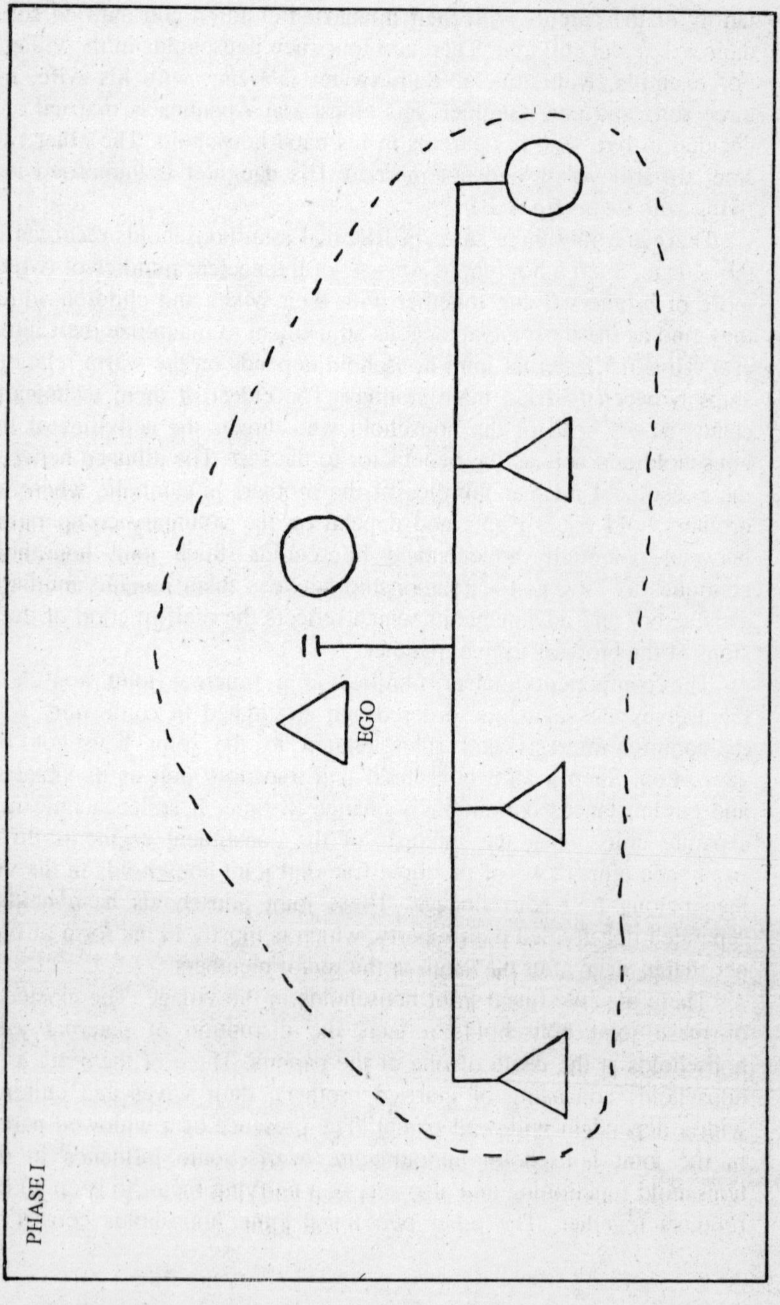

PHASE I

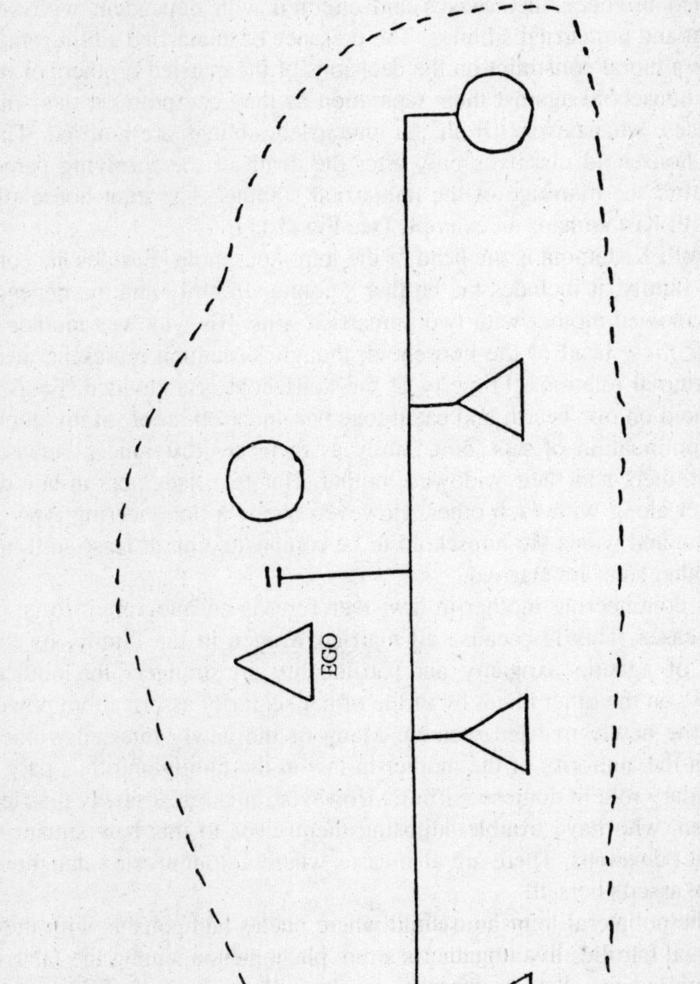

FIG. 4.10 : *Composition of Paternal Joint Household of Kantumuchu Ramaswami*

married brothers, their wives and children with dependent widowed parent and unmarried siblings. The presence of unmarried siblings may act as a moral constraint on the decisions of the married brothers of the joint household against their separation as they compromise their differences, whatsoever, till all the unmarried siblings are married. This joint household dissolves only after the death of the surviving parent and after the marriage of the unmarried siblings. The joint household of Nolli Kistamma is an example (see Fig. 4.11).

Nolli Kistamma is the head of the joint household. Besides his conjugal family, it includes his brother's conjugal family and his dependent widowed mother with two unmarried sons. His widowed mother is the *de facto* head of the household, though Kistamma represents it in its external relations. Property of the household is undivided. Food is prepared on one hearth and eaten together under one roof. Many doubt the continuation of this joint family as there are differences between the brothers and their widowed mother. Her two daughters-in-law do not get along with each other. However, she is a domineering type of woman and wants the household to be composite unit at least until her two other sons are married.

A domineering mother-in-law, therefore, is an integrating force in such cases. This is because all married women in the family, by the rules of agnatic exogamy and patrilocality, are strangers, the mother-in-law, on the other hand, by virtue of her seniority asserts more power than the newly married women. Many of the newly married women accept the authority of the mother-in-law in the family and thus paly a secondary role in domestic affairs. However, in cases of newly married women, who have trouble adjusting themselves to this new situation, conflict develops. There are also cases where a domineering daughter-in-law asserts herself.

The collateral joint household where uncles and cousins with their conjugal families live together is a rare phenomenon among the Jalaris. The only case that is recorded in the village is that of Kasarapu Gurrayya's household which is incidentally the largest family in the village with twelve members (see Fig. 4.12).

Kasarapu Gurrayya is the head of the family. His elder brother's son Tatayya has been the *de facto* head of the household. The family consists of Gurrayya with his wife and his two married sons, their wives and children, along with Tatayya, his wife and a daughter. This is the only case where agnatically related cousins live together under one roof and form an independent economic unit. Tatayya's father,

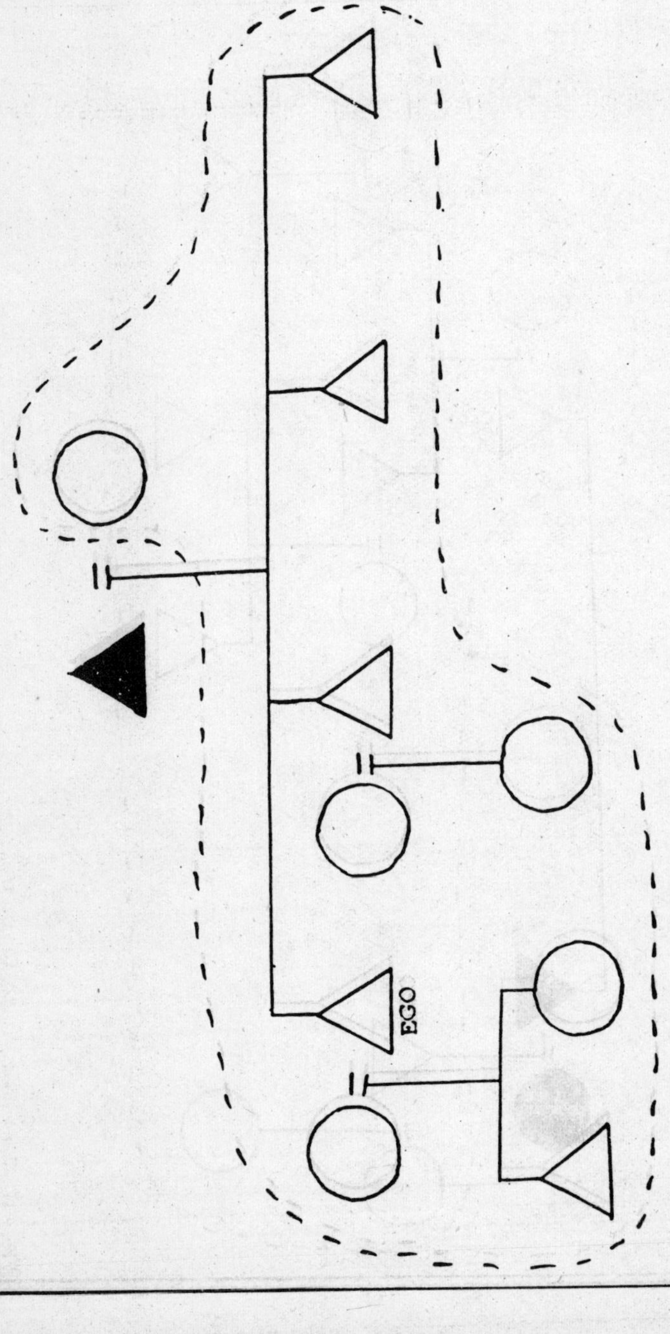

FIG. 4.11 : *Composition of Lineal Joint Household*

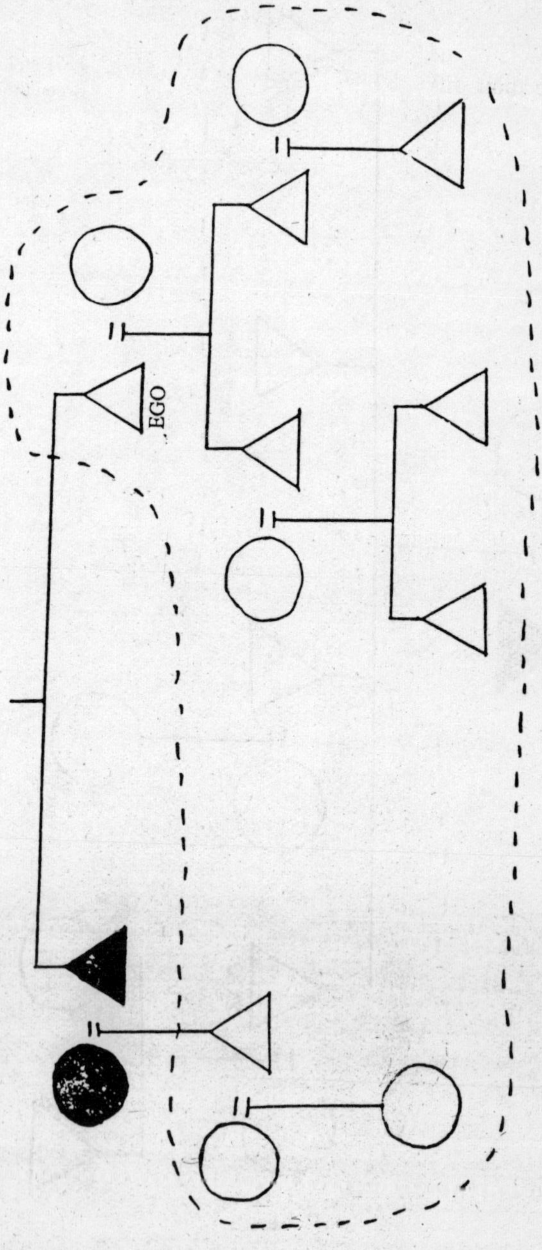

FIG. 4.12 : *Composition of Collateral Joint Household*

who was the head of the family, was dead when Tatayya was very young. His uncle brought him up and got him married. Gurrayya treated his brother's son as his son; he would even say that Tatayya is his eldest son. Tatayya has great respect for his uncle and his wife. His cousins, sons of Gurrayya, too treat him as their 'eldest sibling' and there is no difference among them. When Gurrayya retired voluntarily due to old age he handed over the household responsibilities to his next senior. Tatayya, being the senior member of the family, took over as the head of the household. There are no quarrels and conflicts between the mother-in-law and the daughter-in-law nor among the daughters-in-law.

The property of the household is undivided. They have their own nets and boats and all the three cousins with three others form a net-group of their own and go for fishing. Further, they have shares in the big-net of their lineage. Theirs is one of the richest households in the village. Tatayya and his cousins give their daily earnings to the mother and she looks after the domestic affairs, with the help of Tatayya's wife. Tatayya has no sons and has only one daughter who is grown up for marriage. Gurayya's elder son has two children, one boy and a girl, and the other son has one male child.

In this case, the incentives to the component nuclear families, though different, are identically linked with the maintenance of a joint household. The fact that Tatayya has no male heir is probably a factor that makes Gurrayya's sons remain in the undivided family. When somebody advised Tatayya to adopt a son he seems to have said that his cousin's sons are like his own sons and he is happy with them. Tatayya is not very much interested in as to what will happen to his property after his death. His main aim is to get his daughter a good husband. He has good personal prestige in the community, being the head of a large, wealthy family, which seems to be an incentive that makes him decide to live with his uncle and cousins.

To sum up, the above analysis show that every adult Jalari male encounters with a choice where he has to take a decision whether to separate from his natal household or to remain with it in the event of his marriage. Such a choice is invariably determined by the resources an individual possesses and his maximising capabilities. The Jalari culture recognizes the right of a married male to demand for a separation which is considered normal and an approved practice of the society. The relationship between one's resources and these values are crucial in generating the complex forms of genealogical structures as they determine the kind of decision one makes in the light of these alternatives, i.e., joint living or separate living. Therefore, separation of a household is a normal occurrence in the Jalari society rather than a symptom of disintegration and is a consequence of the dictates of the conditions of world of necessity. But what is disapproved by the Jalaris is not the separation from one's natal household but the timing of separation and one's failure to perform and conform to the 'codes of conduct'.

REFERENCES

1. The implication is that all members of a particular household cook from the same hearth and eat together. This is locally expressed as *oke kunda vanta*. Such a practice of equating the domestic group with the hearth seems to be widespread (see Madan 1965: 45; Berreman 1963: 144; Yalman 1967: 103).
2. The Jalaris also take into consideration a hearth as a household and an independent unit for purposes of collection of contribution for village festivals.
3. A Peddillu is the lineage shrine where the lineage deities are kept and worshipped by its members. It is considered as a sacred place and the lineage priest usually lives in that house observing various taboos related to the sacred nature of the house.
4. Patrilocal residence is the normal and proper rule of residence. Matrilocality among the Jalaris is considered as improper and unusual as it does not belong to the social reality.
5. Nuclear family is used here as a genealogical construct (see Murdock 1948) consisting of "a man and his wife and their child or chilren; household, on the other hand, is treated here as a domestic group", that is a group of persons who at a particular time are living together in one dwelling, or collection of dwellings, with some sort of economic arrangement that may be called a joint house (see Radcliffe Brown 1952: 53). The term extended nuclear family household is being used here to designate a domestic group consisting of a nuclear family and one or more lineal and/or fraternal dependent relatives. The term joint household is retained here for a domestic group of two or more nuclear families.
6. Fortes' concept of developmental cycle of domestic groups as employed in his study of Tallensi (1948) is useful for an understanding of family processes. However, it is not free from criticism (see for example, Barth 1966 : 2). Most recently, Shah (1973) has examined and modified the concept of developmental cycle of domestic groups and proposed a more complex process of change in place of unidirectional process of development.
7. Several studies have shown a close relationship between economic factors and the household composition. Castes and individuals with considerable property tend to retain joint households and among the poorer castes and individuals the household has a shorter life span (see for details Gough 1956: Cohn 1961: Mandelbaum 1972: 47-54).

8. Several authors have noted that quarrel among women of a domestic family is a widespread phenomenon. "The relationship between the various women in a joint family is frequently one of conflict..." (Srinivas 1952: 546). See also Dube (1955: 155) and Madan (1965: 170). "Partitions... are usually the result of quarrels between the men or women of the joint household", (Mayer 1960: 241).
9. There are different classifications of joint families made by several authors. For instance, Madan (1962c) makes a distinction between patrilineal and paternal extended family on the basis of their implications to the family property. However, the classification made in this work is done with reference to the genealogical relations present in the joint household rather than its implication to the joint household property.

FIVE

MAINTENANCE AND REPLACEMENT

THE PRECEDING chapter has outlined the differential occurrence of genealogical composition of the households in Jalaripalem. It was also noted that each household grows and develops in time as a consequence of the social situations created by such social events as birth, marriage and death with alternatives to choose between 'joint living', or 'separate living' from the natal household. These choices and decisions exercised by the Jalaris reveal patterns of regularities of behaviour, i.e. the patterns of events of transactions in which they engage, affecting the composition of the households belong to the realm of social structural reality. This chapter is devoted to present an analysis of the activities of the Jalari household, its organization and specific processes of its maintenance and replacement.

DOMESTIC ORGANIZATION

There is considerable division of labour among members of the household by sex and age. Domestic work and fish marketing fall to the exclusive purview of women, while fishing, repairing the equipment and other odd jobs that require physical strength are taken care of by male members.

A basic division of labour exists between husband and wife. The husband is primarily responsible for supporting the family economically and the wife is responsible for household work and child care. Thus, each partner makes a specialised contribution to the working of family organization.[1] But within the general framework of division of labour, there is considerable variation between the roles of husband and wife. For example, there are instances where a few male members spend away their money on drinking and do not even go for fishing regularly to earn for their families. In such cases, their wives are compelled by circumstances to take up the task of maintenance of the family. Women contribute extensively to family income by taking fish to the nearby markets for sale. In all such cases the grown-up female child of the family takes up the responsibility for domestic work.

Every adult male earns his money by going for fishing as it is the only occupation. Women cannot perform men's tasks such as fishing. Men, on the other hand, cannot do household work such as cooking. In fact, they do not think of doing such jobs since it is not their job and is considered shameful. The villagers ridicule those who do such odd jobs. A man who cooks his own meal is an odd person, though the exception is a widower of the village who cooks for himself. Men also make it clear that they are incapable of handling money since they are not aware of the needs of the household. They believe that the women know better and concede that they are very careful in spending. For this reason, men usually give all or greater part of their earnings to their wives for the maintenance of the household. They take money from their wives whenever they need for their personal expenses. In a joint household, the mother takes control of the household expenditure and her sons hand over their earnings to her and not to their wives.

When dependent members, such as an old widowed parent or siblings, are included in a household they assume secondary roles in the domestic organisation. If the aged father is added to the nuclear family of his son and is not economically active, he ceases to function as the effective head of the family, though he is consulted on matters of ritual and political importance. On the contrary, a widowed mother relatively enjoys considerable status and also plays an active role in the domestic organisation. Most of these widowed mothers usually engage in selling raw and dried fish in the nearby markets contributing substantially to the family income. Daughter-in-law, on the other hand, assumes a secondary role by performing mainly household duties and child care.

All the Jalari households have a recognized head (*yajamani*) who manages the household affairs. He represents his household in all its external relations with other households, lineage heads and strangers. Though the head of the household exercises authority and takes final decisions with respect to domestic and familial spheres, the Jalari adult men and women are almost free to express their opinion. Decisions on matters connected with kinship and marriage, training of children and that affect the family's relations with its agnates and affines are all taken jointly by the spouses and other adult members of the household.[2] Internal authority pattern in the Jalari households exhibits much variation. For formal purposes, however, decisions are made public by the head of the household and his acts alone represent decisions of the household.

The general pattern and sources of power in the family are derived mainly from the concepts and meanings related to the process of incorporation. The idiom of kinship with its primary distinctions of generation, sex and age provides symbols for socialisation of the young and maintenance of order. Subordination and super-ordination are based on juniority and seniority of birth.

Distribution of authority in the households of Jalaripalem is a direct expression of the differential occurrence of genealogical composition of the households. There is no specific correlation of authority with familial kinship roles. In the households of incomplete families, the senior woman of the household exercises authority and on occasions she is represented by a close male relative. However, in many nuclear families, the husband/father is the head of the household and consequently exercises authority. In all these situations, we find that both organizational and kinship values are clustered together. One has to draw a distinction between authority patterns based on relationships of kinship and relationships based on management of household resources. This distinguishes cultural sphere from the social structural sphere of the household organization.

Thus, we find significant variations in the distribution of authority patterns in the composition of extended families and joint families in Jalaripalem village. In many of the extended nuclear families which include a man, his wife and children, his dependent aged and widowed parent and siblings it is the adult son of the family who acts as the head of the household. Likewise, in all the joint families of the village, we see that it is not particularly father or husband in the household who exercises authority but it is the senior person who manages and controls the resources of the household, may he be the grand-father, father's brother, father, elder brother or a cousin.

ANCESTOR WORSHIP

A household not only functions as a separate social and political unit but also functions as an independent religious unit. However, a household acts as a separate religious unit from its natal family only after the death of its senior male member and after the formal division of the natal family. In a joint household, the senior male member acts as an intermediary between ancestors and living members of the family. In certain situations two or more households of a common ancestor (father or grand-father of a family) may join together and act as a religious unit for purposes of ancestor worship. But the tendency and the common practice among the Jalaris is to establish one's own ancestral shrine in his house as an independent religious unit when he is not worshipping his ancestors with his brothers and cousins.

The ancestral shrine (*gondillu*) is situated in the corner of the living room of a house by separating it with a thin mud wall. It is not used for daily habitation.[3] The corner of the ancestral shrine is plastered with turmeric paste and symbols are made of vermillion powder representing ancestors recently dead and others who are unknown. Turmeric paste is applied to the wall in a circle which is divided into two parts by a vertical line of lime powder. Symbols made of vermillion on the left represent unknown ancestors, who are collateral agnates, and theii wives, while on the right represent ancestors of recent past, i.e., known lineal relatives such as grand-parents, parents and children. They offer food and prayers by name to the deceased grand-parents, siblings and other known members of the family during the ancestor worship; and another prayer is collectively offered to all unknown ancestors. The ancestors to whom they offer food and prayers include wives of the deceased agnates who bore children for the family, besides male and unmarried female agnates.

Ancestor worship is considered a moral obligation of the living persons to the dead. Ancestors are worshipped during all major events of the family life, such as birth, marriage, etc. However, it is customary to conduct rituals for the ancestors on every *sankranthi* (14th January of every year) festival without fail.[4] New clothes are purchased and offered to the ancestors on the occasion. Food and fruits are offered in the name of the ancestors, incense is burnt and ancestors are invoked for their blessings.

Every household which keeps its own *gondillu* performs the rituals for ancestor worship under the supervision of the head of the household. He acts as an intermediary between the ancestors and the members of his family as well as a priest of the domestic shrine. His wife is also given an equally important role in the ancestor worship and performs the ritual along with her husband.[5]

The Jalaris not only recognize the close connection between the worship of ancestors and filial piety, but also regard this as their duty (*dharma*) to the family. The Jalaris owe a debt to ancestors of the family and the family in general for the gift of life and sustenance. Failure in the performance of ancestor worship is to undermine the values and ideas of incorporation on which their family group is based and it is regarded as an act of violation of codes of conduct. Obligations on the part of the living members to their parents do not terminate when death removes the latter from among the living. The dead must be brought back to the home and must be 'integrated' with the other ancestors of the family, thereby keeping a continuity between the dead and the living of the family. The Jalaris believe that the ancestors generally do not punish the living members of their family and similarly on their part descendants should not neglect them. The Jalaris take the maximum care to see that their ancestors are not displeased. It is also believed that the ancestors will protect the living kinsmen.

HOUSEHOLD ECONOMY

Household Economy among the Jalaris is sustained by marine fishing and its related activities whereby the Jalari households function and maintain themselves as separate and independent economic units. To be viable, therefore, the Jalaris have devised certain economic arrangements. This is achieved by the active participation of all the adult males of the village in activities of big-nets and other net-groups.

There are two categories of fishermen in the village. They are : owner-fisherman (*sonthadaru*) who owns the fishing equipment and the worker-fisherman or share-cropper (*raithu*) who works in a net-group on the basis of sharing the total catch as remuneration for his labour. However, such a classification is not absolute. The owner-fisherman is also simultaneously a worker-fisherman in the net-group he organizes, but in addition he enjoys the rent derived on the use of his fishing equipment — a benefit the others do not enjoy.

There are 36 households in the village which solely derive their income from the participation of their adult males as worker-fishermen only in big-net and other net-groups. They do not own any productive capital such as nets and boats for fishing operations. Womenfolk of these households sell fresh fish daily in the town markets and dried fish in the weekly markets of the neighbouring villages to supplement their household incomes.

In addition to the earnings of their adult males as worker-fishermen, there are 32 households which derive income by way of rents on their fishing equipment. They own nets and boats and some of them control rights of ownership in big-nets.[6] Seven other households organize their own net-groups and the crew consists of the members of their family with exclusive rights of ownership on fishing equipment.

The remaining two households, with no male adults, earn their income mainly by retail fish trading.

The Jalaris regard all income as the joint income of the household. Income from ownership of boats and nets or fishing activity and fish trading by women is usually considered not as outcome of any individual member's sole efforts, but as belonging to the household itself. An individual earner is always a co-resident with other members of his household. Such a person gives all his income to the head of the household. His income is known to all the members of the household and it is not possible for him to retain a part of it. He is not expected to have any needs which the household does not know of. Every adult male is expected to contribute to household income to the best of his ability, and what he receives is determined by his needs and the available resources.

Household income, however, is not determined by the size of the household alone. An average family, in general, may contain one adult male as its chief earning member. In some cases, the women of the household supplement household income up to two rupees a day by selling fish. But this is not the case with all the households. Some extended nuclear families and joint families have more income due to the existence of more than one adult male and control of fishing equipment.[7] These two factors are complementary. We have already noted the property (in the form of nets and boats) interest of the Jalari individuals is an important determinant that influences the composition of the households. Consequently the majority of these households in the village derive income either by virtue of having two or more adult males or by controlling the ownership of the fishing equipment. There is thus a relationship between household composition, ownership of boats and nets and household incomes. Table 5.1 represents the variation in the household incomes among the fishermen of Jalaripalem.

Table 5.1: Distribution of Household Incomes for the Year 1968-69

Annual income (approximate)	*Number of households*
Rs. 650 - 900	36
Rs. 901 - 1200	24
Rs.1201 - 1500	12
Rs.1501 - 1800	5

Yearly income of two households, whose heads are women, is estimated at about Rs. 650 each which is very low. They derive this income mainly by selling fish every day in the nearby markets. Other lower income households derive their incomes mainly through the sole efforts of an individual fisherman, and in a few cases it is supported by the earnings of the women.

The households which earned more than Rs. 1200 per year are both nuclear and extended families, including some joint families. Highest income in the village Rs. 1800 was earned by the joint household belonging to Kasarapu lineage consisting of twelve members. Its sources of income ranged from fishing, renting of fishing equipment and through the control of big-net shares.

The pattern of domestic spending is standardized among the Jalari. Further, it is noticed that a high income is not reflected much in their living standards. Principal items of household expenditure are common for all the households. They consist usually of the following items:

1. Food : *chodi* (ragi), *jonna* (jowar) and *vari* (paddy),
2. Firewood for cooking and kerosene for lighting,
3. Clothing (thrice a year),
4. Utensils,
5. Recreation, entertaining guests and drinks,
6. Medicines, doctors and lineage priests to cure illness,
7. Travelling,
8. House construction, repairs and improvements,
9. Domestic rituals related to life cycle and lineage deities,
10. Gift to married female agnates and other affines.

As much as 70 per cent of the income is spent on food. The Jalaris eat twice a day and their food consists of gruel made of ragi/jowar/millet. Only during nights they eat cooked rice with fish curry. However, the high earning households may supplement gruel with cooked rice in their afternoon meal. They may exhibit their economic well-being in the performance of marriage rituals and ceremonies. In short, the spending patterns of the household expenditure of the rich and the poor Jalaris are considerably similar. Surplus wealth of the high income households is usually converted into gold to be used for hard days during the lean fishing season.

The above picture of the Jalari household economy and standards of living confirms the view that an average Jalari household lives at subsistence level. Since fishing economy is a labour intensive activity, the main source of income is derived by an adult fisherman of the household. Though some households own fishing equipment, which is a source of additional income, every other household derives, invariably, its income mainly by day's hard work of its male members on the open sea. Rough estimate of an average income of an adult fisherman is about rupees three only and most of the households fall into this category. However, another rupee or two may be supplemented by woman of the family by a daily selling of fish at the nearby markets. But, this is not true of all households and is valid so far as the worker-fisherman households are concerned. In case of the households with more adult males and with control of fishing equipment the women stay at home which is a matter of prestige as well as an indicator of economic well being of those households.

The low level of technology and the nature of insecurity involved in the fishing expeditions make their economy precarious. Fishermen's households have, therefore, low standard of living in comparison to agricultural castes of this region.

PROPERTY INHERITANCE AND SUCCESSION

When a married Jalari male separates from his natal household and establishes a new family, his family forms a new and independent household. Such formal separation among the Jalaris is not simply a division of residential and consumption unit, but a formal division of both hearth and property. This new family, thus, not only functions as a distinct social, political, religious and economic unit, but also functions as a distinct property owning unit whereby a Jalari develops his exclusive private assets. We shall describe in the following the standard Jalari arrangements, i.e., the cultural rules and strategies whereby rights of household property are regulated and transmitted.

Household Property

Household property generally consists of corporeal property only. Incorporeal rights are hereditary rights such as rights of succession to positions of village head (*gramapedda*) lineage head (*pillagadu*) and other religious titles such as the village priest (*dasudu*) and the lineage priest (*bhaktudu*). These rights are transferred or abandoned just as any other corporeal property. Rights are transferred from a father to son, just as household property is transferred.

On the other hand, the head of the household enjoys certain rights over his wife and children. "These are recognized as possessive rights over persons" (Radcliffe-Brown, 1950: 127). The rights of a man over his wife as his sexual partner and house partner of his household; and his rights over his children as his proteges, are well recognized. The Jalari often says that the wife and children are his property (*sottu*). By implication, a Jalari claims ownership of the services and labour of his wife and children. They are owned individually and cannot be inherited, transferred or partitioned.

The Jalaris classify property of the household as immovable and movable. Immovable property consists, of houses, lands, etc. Movable property consists of catamarans, boats, nets, gold, silver, jewellery household furniture and other goods.

Generally, property is held in the form of gold, besides nets and boats. Whenever a Jalari household accumulates enough surplus wealth, it is automatically changed into gold ornaments for the women of the household with implicit understanding that they belong to the household, and not to the particular individuals who adorn them.

In contrast to household property, members of a household have rights over lineage property like *peddillu* (shrine of the lineage deities), the right to worship the lineage deity and to participate in the big-net fishing activity of the lineage. Ownership of big-net rests, in reality, with different senior households of the lineage and every member of the lineage has indirect interest in it. The big-net organisation is controlled by the headman (*pillagadu*) of the lineage as the net belongs to the lineage and not to the individual members or the households.

Household property is jointly owned by agnatically related males of the family. Female members of the household, whether agnatically ralated or married into the family as spouses, do not have the right of ownership to household property. An unmarried woman however, has the right to maintenance in her natal household and after marriage she acquires this right in her conjugal family. Further, the Jalaris concede that when a woman's husband deserts her or is dead, she has the right to live in her husband's joint family, but she has the option to stay on either with her conjugal family or to go back to natal household if she wishes so. Thus she has the right to maintenance both in her natal household and her conjugal family. The decision as to where she wants to stay is generally influenced by certain factors. If she has children and property to look after, she stays usually with her conjugal family so as to preserve and safeguard the rights of her children. She acts as a custodian to her children. If she is still young and wants to marry again, she returns to her natal family.

Only in exceptional cases, a widowed or deserted woman goes to her natal family with her children to settle there. In such cases, the children of the woman are reared at her natal household. However, her children have no rights on her natal family and do not inherit her father's or brother's property.

If a woman is deprived of the right to maintenance by her conjugal family at the death of her husband or due to the reluctance of her husband's brothers to give her male children their legal share of her husband's property, she has every right to demand either for her own maintenance or to safeguard the rights of her male children. However, she has no right to transfer the property of her deceased husband from his joint family. The following case illustrates further the right to maintenance of a widowed woman. In 1958, Chintapalli Bhooloka's daughter Muttemma was married to her classificatory father's sister's son. Bhooloka was then living with his wife and two sons. Since she was the only daughter, Bhooloka was very affectionate towards her. However, her husband died soon after her marriage. Members of her husband's household blamed Muttemma as one who brought ill-luck to the family. Consequently, she left her husband's household and returned to her natal family. Later, she was persuaded to go and live with her conjugal household when her husband's brothers agreed to concede her right to maintenance on her husband's share of the family property.

The normal rule of post-marital residence among the Jalari is patrilocal. However, a woman with strained relations with her husband or his relatives usually returns to her natal household and is not allowed to go back to her husband till the relations improve. In such cases, it is the duty of the woman's father and brothers to give her shelter and also help improve her relations with her conjugal family till they come to an agreement.

Kantumuchu Appanna's daughter Danamma was married in the year 1965. Her relations with her husband and the other members of her conjugal family were not good. She never stayed continuously for more than a month in her conjugal household. Her parents and brothers persuaded her to return to her husband's household. Though her parents tried to settle the problem through the mediation of the elders of the community yet, her father was not successful in convincing his daughter to go back to her husband's household once again or her husband's parents to take her back. Later, she married another man thus forfeiting her right to maintenance in her former husband's household.

Inheritance and Succession

Patrimony is inherited by sons and so long as a household continues to exist, the question of succession does not arise. A birth or adoption of a male member in the household diminishes the beneficial interests of the survivors and death, on the other hand, enlarges the beneficial interests of the survivors. When division of patrimony takes place, the property of the household is divided equally among the male members, one share each to the coparceners. If the division of property takes place during the life time of a father, an equal share is retained by him towards his maintenance. After the death of the father, theoretically the sons have joint claims on his share of the property, but normally it goes to the youngest son with whom the father was staying after separation, as revealed in a number of cases collected.

When division takes place after the death of a father all his sons divide the entire property equally among themselves. Similarly, when a person dies without leaving a son or his wife behind him, his property is divided among his collateral agnates, that is, his brother's male children. Seniority of birth has no claims for preferential treatment in the division of property of the household.

The younger brother of Kadiri Krishna Murthy, the present headman of the village, died without any children, leaving behind considerable property. His property was inherited by his brother's sons, who are considered as legal heirs, after the death of his wife.

The household of Kadiri Achanna, his brother Satteyya and cousin Pentayya (FBS) was undivided. They lived together in a joint household till the death of their fathers. This was an undivided property of their fathers who were brothers. This property consisted of two catamarans, two *irugola* and four other types of nets including shares in the big-net. The property was first divided into two parts, one each to their deceased fathers, one half of that property was exclusively inherited by Pentayya as his share of his patrimony and the other half was further divided into two equal shares, between Atchanna and Satteyya, as patrimony. This shows that the surviving members of a joint property held-in-corporation do not inherit and succeed equally as coparceners; but what they inherit and succeed equally is the patrimony (see Fig. 5.1). Inheritance and succession, therefore, are situational and the extent of a share is determined by the composition of the joint household.[8] The principle implied here is that each individual gets an equal share of the patrimony which is an exclusive private asset of the father.

Partition of the Household

The question of partition of property does not arise so long as adult men live together with their wives and children under the authority of their father or any other senior male member. In a joint household, the Jalaris maintain their joint property and live as a single unit. The maintenance of a joint household property is directly related to the mutual consent and the inter-dependence of the constituent members of the household with common rights and obligations as well as with the general satisfaction of their personal interests. The moment it is felt that a father is favouring one son against another and injustice is being done, differences arise and the chances of conflict and cleavage in the household become real, though they may not become overt in the life time of a father.

In such cases, he may remedy the situation before it becomes too explosive by letting the aggrieved son to separate and establish his own independent household without formal partition of the property. More often, the aggrieved son waits for his time and refrains from coming into an open conflict with his father as he cannot risk the general disapproval of his behaviour in the community as it amounts to violation of the code of conduct.

What we find empirically is that sons rarely ask for partition of the patrimony when the father is alive, for patrimony is recognized and considered as the exclusive private property of a person. It is the father who has to take a decision regarding partition of the property in such situations. Therefore, there is some uncertainties involved in coming into open conflict with one's father by going against his wishes. The aggrieved son usually plays safe and separates from the natal household without demanding partition of the household property and establishes his independent household. This arrangement would give an adult son an opportunity to develop his private assets and postpone his claim on the share of his father's property.

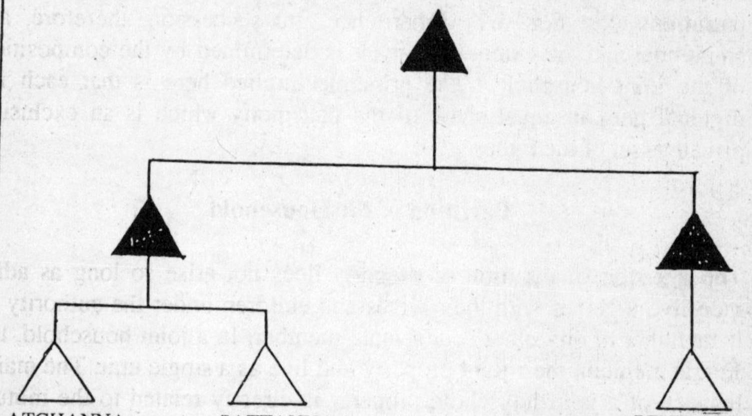

FIG. 5.1 : *Inheritance and Succession of Patrimony among Cousins*

It is, therefore, rarely that there is a partition immediately after the marriage. The cultural rules and strategies in this matter are very clear. In ideal conditions, it is not until the father is dead and at least not until all the brothers are married that partition takes place. In the realm of social structural reality, on the other hand, partition may occur during the life time of a father with unmarried male children or immediately after his death as revealed in the case of histories of almost all the households in the village.

If a joint household survives a division after the marriages of its sons, the situation in the household after the father's death, however, changes drastically and division usually takes place. Each brother seeks to protect the interests of his wife and children, i.e., his conjugal family, and by doing so he comes into open conflict with his brothers. Joint living is ideal up to the point it serves the interests of the constituent partners, but conflict of interests between them becomes usually so persistent as to be beyond compromise. Therefore, division of a joint household is considered a normal; occurrence in the Jalari society.

Causes of Partition

The basic cause for a division of property is conflict between members of the joint household. Conflicts arise out of situation that prevails in both the paternal and fraternal joint families. The joint households consists of several conjugal families which are related through agnatic bond. Conflicts in a paternal joint household is minimised to a certain extent due to the presence of the father as the unilineal ideology of obedience and with a symmetrical relationship of super-ordination and subordination that act as constraints. In a joint household there are feelings of uneasiness and bickerings between brothers over the allocation of household resources. At the same time, as sons of the same father and as co-parceners, they hold equal rights over the property. Again, between a father and a son there are defined rights and obligations which make each other inter-dependent. On the other hand, sibling solidarity cannot sustain if brothers differ in their personal interests in the world of necessity. This breaks the fraternal joint household after the death of the father.

"Conflicts among brothers arise due to their wives who play on these differences" (Madan, 1965 : 170). Daughters-in-law are put under the control and supervision of the mother-in-law. But when she dies they come under the control of the wife of the eldest son of the household. The other daughters-in-law of the family may not like the elevation of one of them to the status of mistress of the household, and try to assert their equality. When there are more than two daughters-in-law in a household, they have disagreements with each other, though they sometimes form temporary alliances.

The main reason for differences between daughters-in-law is that within the sphere of joint household organization the rights and role-expectations are not clearly defined and each appears as a competitor to the other. Each daughter-in-law of the joint household wants her independence and wants to be the mistress of her own home. The attitude of a woman towards her sisters-in-law in a fraternal joint family sometimes may be influenced by her rights and independence rather than to be submissive.[9] Even if there are occasional quarrels between sisters-in-law they do not lead to partition. Actually, it is the involvement of the brothers that leads to a partition; and quarrels act as only complementary factors. They become, however, important in deciding partition only when the sibling solidarity is weakened.

To summarise a major feature of the Jalari family system that affects the household composition and its division is its patrilineal character in which a distinction is made between the positions of males and females in terms of their rights and role expectations. In matters of inheritance and succession, the rights of male members of a household are recognized and given importance to the exclusion of its female members. The female members of a household whether they are agnatically related or married into the family as spouses do not have the rights of ownership to the household property. An unmarried woman, however, has the right to maintenance in her natal household as identical to that of her brothers. The normal practice among the Jalaris is that on the event of marriage, a girl leaves her natal household and takes up residence at her husband's household. The obligation for her maintenance is transferred, after her marriage, to her conjugal family. She, however, retains her right to maintenance in her natal household as expressed in the form of prestations on various specified occasions. When a woman becomes a widow or is deserted by her husband, she has the option either to stay on with her conjugal family or to return to her natal household.[10] On the other hand, the male members of the household, vested with culturally recognized rights of inheritance, assert their right for separation from the household and try to maximize their resources and values.

Separation from the household does not arise so long as adult men live together with their wives and children under the authority of their father or any other senior male member. In such a joint household, the Jalaris maintain their common interests and joint rights and live as a single unit. To certain extent, maintenance of a joint household is directly related to inter-dependence of the constituent members of the household with mutual rights and obligations and general satisfaction of their personal interests. The moment a son thinks that his father favours one son against another and injustice is being done to him, differences are bound to arise and the chances of conflict and cleavage in the household become real, though they may not culminate into a division of the property in the life time of father.

INTER-PERSONAL RELATIONSHIPS

Basic kinship relations are expressed in terms of husband-wife relationship, parent-child relationship, based upon marriage, opposition between the adjacent generations, and between siblings based upon patrilineal descent and equality of status. They also reflect the attitudes and sentiments among the familial kin and thus form a single system by itself. Behaviour of each person is part of the system since his acts upto a measure influence the subsequent behaviour of the other members in the family. In the following, ideal patterns of behaviour between the members of the family are discussed.

Wife and Husband

Close and intimate relationship is expected between wife and husband and is an essential feature of the Jalari family life. Common interests and recognition of authority of the husband over his wife are the factors that bring them closer as years pass by. Systematic relations between wife and husband are not static, but grow with age of the couple and have multifarious dimensions at different phases of family life.

On marriage, a man's relation with his wife is restricted as he lives in his natal household with his parents, married brothers and other unmarried siblings. Though a man's exclusive rights and responsibilities over his wife are recognized, it is his household that is regarded and treated as responsible in matters of relations between the wife and husband by the wife's parents. This, however, is the case in the initial stages of the marriage. Likewise, a woman's activities are restricted in the joint family set-up and she is not expected to look after the interests of her husband alone. In such situations, the interests of the wife and husband to each other are repressed and the interests of the joint household are emphasized and given importance. Thus, the only exclusive interests the young couple have in their early married life are as sexual partners. Sexual gratification is regarded as an essential feature of a successful marriage. With birth of children a woman ends her status as an affine in her conjugal family and her status in the family of her husband changes drastically.

Birth of children fulfills the ultimate objective of their life and family becomes complete. Their inclusion into the family have implications for husband-wife relations which marks the second phase in the development of the relationship. Children give them a sense of security as they become the centre of their common interests and activities of the family. This makes the relationship stronger and the wife will be the most unwilling to leave her husband, however hard her life may be.

As years pass by, greater familiarity between wife and husband eventually leads to greater intimacy. A woman identifies herself with the interests of her husband and they show devotion and affection for each other. This is reflected in the confidence of a man in his wife in the discussions of important domestic matters and both of them take decisions, though the final decision rests with the husband.

The husband-wife relationship that starts with an exclusive sexual connotation becomes more complex with the addition of other interests, rights and obligations. Though the relationship grows stronger in time, relative independence also emerges as a woman grows old. After the birth of her children her role as a wife weakens and her role as mother dominates the family activities. Her attention is directed more to the welfare of the children.

Parents and Children

Parents love their children and they are the supreme objects of their love and affection. The father, as the head of the household, acts as an authoritarian and controls their actions. He also controls the wealth of the household, but uses it to provide the children with proper clothing, food, shelter, tools and other necessities. The mother, though subject to the authority of her husband, has sole charge of the household affairs and provides sustenance during the period of infancy to her children. She also trains her daughter in household work, while the father teaches his son the art of fishing. Thus parents together are responsible for the child's nourishment, education and discipline and have complementary roles to perform.

The Jalari parents also perform some complementary obligations towards their children in various phases of their lives. When children are sick, it is the responsibility of the parents to consult the local doctor or the diviner. It is also the responsibility of the parents to offer sacrifices to the deities and spirits whenever it is necessary.

The Jalari children not only obey their parents, but also respect them, work for them and take their sides against everybody else becasue they are the persons from whom they inherit every thing.[11] "Dependence on one's parents increases the child's attachment and duty towards them. The emphasis is on the parents and they are responsible for the child's well being in social, economic, jural and ritual matters. Conflicts between parents and children are not uncommon, although they never become so acute as between brothers or other agnates.

Brothers and Sisters

Brothers are held together by common descent and common background and interests. The notion of equivalence of siblings of a family is based upon equal social positions, the rights and obligations they inherit by common relationship with their parents, irrespective of senior and junior status of their birth. They belong to the same social class and with implications of equality in their relationship.

Intimacy and close identification of siblings are also rooted in their common dependence on their mother in the childhood. It is on her that they depend for food and emotional security and a mother cares all her children equally. The first lessons of equality of status and rights are learnt in this setting. The unequal status between the elder brother and the younger brother as a kinship idiom manifests only when the seniors act as guardians in the absence of the parents. In turn, however, the juniors show respect and obedience to the older ones. In such cases, the eldest of the male sibling acts as trustee and keeps the property intact by assuming the role of the head of the household.[12]

The first born male child is thus important since he is next in the succession to take the father's role as the head of the household. He even performs the marriages of his younger siblings and accepts the social responsibilities involved in such transactions.

Ties of mutual affection and devotion between siblings last throughout their lives and are extended to their children. Normally, relations between brothers are affective, intimate and close as they share many common interests and hold equal rights as coparceners in the father's property. These relations are continued as long as they live in the natal household and are extended later in normal conditions when they are married and separated.

Conflicts between brothers, however, arise sometimes after they are married and separated from the natal family. The climax of this process sets in with the marriage of the siblings or more accurately after they beget children. This brings in cleavages between siblings, both on the level of jural and economic relations, and thus, is pertinent and made more prominent through the differing interests towards their respective conjugal families. When married brothers live together in a joint household, conflicts between them usually arise in the management of the household, in the distribution of benefits and services and in rearing children. In this situation, close and intimate relations between brothers disappear as they establish their independent households and the familiarity and devotion between them turns into disagreement and antagonism.

The basis of this is the fact that brothers establish their separate households but do not thereby relinquish membership of their family. They still have common interests, rights and obligations in their joint activities. They do not sever the social and personal bonds between the brothers which means that they do not forfeit any of their rights or relinquish any of their obligations as sons and brothers of their natal household.[13] They are independent only to develop their private and truly exclusive assets within the bonds set by the unity of the family and associated rules pertaining to it.

Sisters maintain close relations and stand in much the same kind of relationship that we observe between the brothers. But, unlike the brothers, the sisters, of a natal family, once married are never united again. Sisters maintain their contacts by regularly visiting the natal household. When a sister comes to her natal household for her first confinement other sisters also come to see and help her during pregnancy as well as after the child is born.

A brother is always prepared to support his sister. He treats her kindly when she comes to visit her natal family. Brothers, on such occasions, present her with clothes and other presents. He maintains close contact with her husband and his family by visiting them frequently, with gifts as part of the obligation of the marriage transaction. He also comes to her rescue and allows her to take refuge in his household after domestic disputes. He bears all the obligations that follow the marriage transaction between his natal family and his sister's husband's family, both during the life time of his father and after his death. This makes the relationship between brother and sister affective, close and intimate.

Uncles and Nephews

The other set of inter-personal relations consists of the other agnatic kinsmen living in a joint household which includes uncles and nephews, cousins and grand parents and grand children of agnatic kinship in the extended and joint households. The most important relations a Jalari experiences are those with his paternal uncles and cousins. The father's brother and brother's son relationship is epitomized by father-son relationship in which opposition between the senior and junior generations are expressed. The Jalari emphasises an element of inequality in their relationship generally characterized by the authority and super-ordination of father's brother and dependence and subordination of a brother's son. Though effective relations and sentiments are expressed through co-residence and co-operation in work, authoritarian role of the father's brother is not easily reconcilable with any free interaction between them.

Father's brother is classified and included in the broad category of father and is addressed either as elder to father (*pedababu*) or as younger to father (*chinababu*) to differentiate him from one's father. However, father's brother and brother's son relationship lacks intimacy and personal obligations of the father-son relationship. Therefore, a father's brother only can ask for his help in performing various tasks, but cannot direct or demand of his brother's son as his own.

The importance of father's brother is well recognized by the Jalari and this is evident by the statement that he is a kinsman who is a co-resident of one's natal family (*oke kutumbamuloni manishi*) and who had split from his brother's household. Father's brother takes active part and shows interest in the affairs of his brother's son. He defends and safeguards the interests of his brother's son against others in matters related to family honour and respect. On the other hand, a man approaches his father's brother rather instead his affines for advice, help and co-operation.

The Jalaris also recognize latent and inherent antagonism between a father's brother and brother's son, stemming from the belief that the paternal uncle regards his brother's son as a rival to his own son in relation to paternal property. Therefore, rivalries and conflicts between them are also common.

To a significant extent, attitudes and feelings are canalized into a relationship of less intimacy and warmth between uncle and nephew. However, we must recognize that though latent rivalry and conflict are present in their relationship, it does not totally tend to deteriorate. Nor can we say that it is all antagonism rather than co-operation and mutual assistance. Still, the essential unity and solidarity of the agnatic kin are maintained and brother's sons do not contest the authority of their father's brothers. On many occasions they co-operate and help each other. Importance of the father's brother is well recognized especially in matters related to property, legal affairs and religious matters.

Relations between Cousins

When we move from the consideration of relationships between members of proximate generations to relations between agnates of the same generation, we find a significant emphasis on equality. The relationships of agnates of the same generation are characterized by lack of formality that we observe between agnates of proximate generations. Agnatic cousins are regarded as brothers and sisters as they grow together and reside in the neighbourhood and are usually playmates in childhood. Agnatic cousins help each other and are bound together by common background, identity and interests which they share in their corporate descent group.

A man regards his agnatic cousins as important advisers and helpers in such matters as marriages, etc. His cousins advise and help him as members of his own generation and his descent group. The relations between agnatic cousins are close and intimate and are more free than with their fathers and father's brothers. In times of quarrels and disputes with affines and outsiders, it is the agnatic cousins who come to rescue and defend him from others.

Agnatic cousins act together whenever need arises even though they live separately. But the position with regard to distant cousins is variable and changes from case to case depending upon the intensity of the genealogical nearness. The closer the relationship, the more intense the interaction between them, with mutual expectations of rights and obligations. The tendency is for gradual loosening of bonds, privileges and obligations between agnatic kinsmen, separated from their common ancestor.

The bonds of agnatic kinship are associated with various obligations. The most important of these is lineage exogamy. The patrilineal ideology and lineage exogamy prohibit marriage between agnatic cousins. They are taught from an early age that sex and marital relations between them are forbidden. Observation of pollution and death mourning is obligatory. It involves absention from bathing, changing clothes and avoidance of rituals and ceremonies. Observance of these for an agnate is a social expectation among the Jalaris.

Similarly, during ceremonies related to birth and marriage, solidarity and differentiation come into prominence between agnates and non-agnates. On such occasions, agnates help each other and cooperate. They provide the much needed help in domestic and other works specific on these occasions, like cooking, distribution of food, entertaining guests and performance of rituals. The day-to-day interactions between the agnatic kin have wider scope. They range from working together on identical tasks to informal mutual visiting, lending and borrowing of articles of domestic use, and helping each other in various kinds of domestic work.

Though hostility between agnatic cousins is recognized as arising out of claims over ancestral property, comradeship and co-operation also characterize their relationship. Potential rivalry between agnatic cousins is a phenomenon found more between agnatic cousins of a joint household rather than between distant agnatic cousins. When a household, in course of its development, enters the phase of a joint family, an incompatibility develops between cousins due to the individual's self-interest, on the one hand, and the expectation of mutual co-operation and loyalty to each other, on the other hand. This rivalry generally leads to partition. After partition, supremacy of personal interest is openly recognized and agnatic cousins deal with each other in terms of their self-interest and on a reciprocal basis. Every act of kindness, help or hospitality is noted and returned when opportunity arises. There is both co-operation as well as conflict between them based on the recognition of equality in status. Siblings rivalry which leads to partition of the household is later revealed in a more intense form in relations between agnatic cousins.

Grand-parents and Grand-children

The essential feature of the relationship between the members of alternate generations of agnates is that of intimacy and mutual trust based upon the recognition of equality between them. Grand-children are frequently named after their paternal grand-parents and addressed as such, and relations between them are exceptionally cordial. There is a pleasant, free and easy relationship between them.

Grand-parents find joy in taking care of their grand-children. After a few weeks of her confinement, the mother of the child resumes her routine household duties and the grand-parents, whether they live in the same household or not, take care of the child in her absence. They also pay a predominant role in rearing the child and the child usually spends most of its time with them after weaning. The child also usually sleeps with one of its grand-parents during the nights.

Grand-parents indulge their grand-children, but they also discipline and instruct them. Whenever a grand-parent gives an order or administers a scolding, it is always something different from a father's discipline. They regard it as a friendly correction and they take it as a piece of advice. So, grand-parents may scold a grand-child, but usually they are kind towards the young children. There are no joking relations between paternal grand-parents and their grand-children, as they are agnatically related to each other and among whom such behaviour is prohibited. On the whole, friendliness involved in the relationships of grand-parents and grand-children signifies equivalence of alternate generations.

REFERENCES

1. Family is treated here as a social system, that is, as a system of interdependent roles, as an organized group carrying out tasks in a particular social environment.
2. Male authoritarianism is often confused with differentiation of conjugal roles. There are no father centred and mother centred families. But both play an important role, for each partner has authority and responsibility in their own spheres.
3. Writing in general about society in India, Mandelbaum observes : "In almost every house there is a special place for the holy things that help guard all in the household" (1972 : 42).
4. *Sankranthi* festival is celebrated by all South Indians and has the features of agricultural society, as it is performed to offer the first crop of the harvest to the ancestors. Though the Jalari economy has no agricultural base, they follow the practice of the larger society.
5. Rites for the family's ancestors are particularly important in all the households. Madan observes among Kashmiri Brahmans that if the family has separated, the eldest brother still must conduct these rites for all (1962b : 14). Gough also states that in Tanjore district each household head must separately carry out this ritual duty (1956 : 839).
6. Most of the senior families belonging to the lineages having big-nets actually control the rights of ownership of big-nets. Generally, these families control most of the eight shares of the big-net and are traditionally wealthy, owing to their advantageous position in the social structure. Others own different varieties of smaller nets and catamarans. One thirds of the total catch is retained by the owners of these nets as rent, who actually organize the net-group. On the other hand, one share, equal to a fisherman's wage, is given for the use of a boat or a catamaran.
7. "The number of men in a family is economically significant because the pooled labour and wealth of several men may give them advantages over a small family" (Mandelbaum 1972 : 44).
8. In joint families where co-residents are brothers, they all equally inherit the household property as it is divided into equal shares. On the other hand, if the joint family consists of cousins, they do not inherit and succeed to equal shares of household property, but inherit and succeed to the patrimony which is divided equally among brothers, as revealed in the cases cited above.
9. However, the Jalari parents never directly participate in the household conflict of their son-in-law. All they can do is to defend their daughter's behaviour in her quarrels with her sisters-in-law.

10. "As long as a man's parents are alive, or there are other elders, particularly males, in the household, his relations with his wife are severely limited. He has no exclusive jural responsibility on her behalf... Similarly, a woman is not expected to do anything for her husband alone, unless, of course, she is the wife of the head of the household" (Madan 1965 : 134).
11. An individual's status in the Jalari society is inherited from his parents. As boy and man, a Jalari treats both his parents with great respect and in an ideal situation, a son devotes himself completely to the welfare as well as to the will of his parents.
12. The roles of elder and younger brothers is generally more marked in the North than in the South. Mayer observes agnatic relations among Ramkeri villagers tend to be formal (1960 : 219). On the other hand, men of *lower jatis* are more likely to emphasize the equality of brothers -- the peer, rather than the unequal relationship (see Mandelbaum 1972 : 64).
13. "The bond between brothers is taken ideally as a durable and cohesive relationship of co-operative action, second only to the tie between father and son" (Mandelbaum 1972 : 66), though estrangement among adult brothers is noted a salient feature of the family system in Kashmir village. (Madan 1965 : 169).

SIX

THE JALARI REVISITED

THE VILLAGE Jalaripalem was revisited in the month of October and again in December 1985 to study the changes that took place since 1969. Several significant changes have been noticed in the lives of the Jalari emanating from shifting of the village from its original habitat. The consequent changes in the life styles of the Jalari in religious, political and economic spheres in general and the changing household structures and family life in particular are discussed briefly below :

JALARIPALEM SINCE 1969

The Original settlement of Jalaripalem was submerged by a severe tidal wave in 1978 and all the dwellings of the village were washed away by sea. Then the Government of Andhra Pradesh came forward to help the Jalaris with financial assistance to construct *pucca* houses on an elevated and safer place. The alternative site for the construction of *pucca* houses was shown at Chinnametta village, situated on a nearby hillock nearer to the sea-shore. Each householder was given a sum of Rs. 12,000 by the Revenue Department of the Government of Andhra Pradesh towards material cost for the construction of houses. The Jalaris themselves contributed their labour and constructed about 150 tiled houses.

But their stay in the rehabilitated colony was very brief, only for a period of three years, as the area south of Balacheruvu backwaters was selected for establishment of a steel project. The village of Jalaripalem, along with its neighbouring villages, was forced to evacuate in 1981 when the construction work of the Visakha Steel Plant started. All the displaced persons belonging to fishermen castes were rehabilitated near Dibbapalem village. The Jalaris were paid a compensation of Rs. 3,000 to 4,000 for each room they lost in the original village of Jalaripalem at Chinnametta at the time of evacuation. The rehabilitation took place in batches.

The first batch of settlers from Jalaripalem came to the Rehabilitation Centre in October, 1982. Register numbers were given to each married Jalari for schemes of housing, including distribution of house sites and money and material for construction, and for preference in employment in the steel plant. The housing scheme for the Jalari included free supply of 50 bags of cement, steel rods and cash of Rs. 12,000 for each householder. The distribution of material and money was done by personnel of Revenue Department Government of Andhra Pradesh.

Almost all the Jalaris complained that the distribution of money and material was very faulty. Some had received only half of the bags of cement that were promised to be delivered to them. The others complained that they did not receive the full quota of cement and the promised money, though in most of the cases they have signed as if they had received Rs. 12,000 and allotted cement bags. In reality, the Jalaris claim, they were given only Rs. 10,000 per head. Not all of them were given these facilities and the householders registered in the second phase were yet to receive any assistance by the time of my visit. In some cases sustenance allowance of Rs. 300 was given. In most cases they complained that they did not get cement and iron rods and were told that they would get them in the second phase. The Government of Andhra Pradesh has implemented only the first phase and the second phase is yet to be started.

There were as many as 225 Jalari young married men with the status of householder registered under this scheme. They were given house sites on the basis of having registration numbers. Widows were also entitled for registration numbers. Each such householder was given a plot of land measuring 107 square yards and a subsidy of Rs. 800 for construction of a hut initially. But later on they were provided with a loan of another instalment of Rs. 12,000 to each married male for construction of *pucca* houses under the second stage.

The second batch of 44 Jalaris was granted registration numbers and allotted house sites for construction of *pucca* houses in the Rehabilitation Centre. They had not yet constructed their houses as money and material were not released to them.

The reconstruction of the Jalaripalem village and the arrangement of *pucca* houses in the Rehabilitation Centre reveal a pattern similar to the one that was observed in the original settlement. Members belonging to a particular descent group, e.g., Chintapilli or Kadiri, have occupied land in a contiguous area as it was in Jalaripalem. In the allotment of house sites also preference was given to lineal kinsmen, such as fathers, sons and brothers, and house sites were allotted side-by-side. Therefore, it is not uncommon to find a particular father and his sons or two or more married brothers constructing a singular house on the house site allotted to them, in the neighbourhood of their agnatic kinsmen, each having an independent dwelling of his own.

However, the division of the village into two halves as *ega veedhi* and *diga veedhi* and the associated organisation are not there at present, though Kasarapu and Kadiri occupy areas in a north-south direction facing each other as it was in the original village.

JALARIPALEM IN 1985

Jalaripalem Village is now an integral part of Dibbapalem Rehabilitation Centre. The Dibbapalem Rehabilitation Centre is situated 20 kms. south of Visakhapatnam town between the villages of Peddagantyada and Dibbapalem, about five kms. north of their original village. The Rehabilitation Centre consists of approximately 5,000 fishermen of the villages of Jalaripalem, Gangavaram, Peda Pallipalem and Chinna Pallipalem (Chinametta) belonging to the Jalari, Vada and Palli castes. The other displaced persons, belonging to Nellimukku, Parvada and other agricultural villages, were rehabilitated in other centres situated at Peddagantyada and Aganampudi villages which are now part of the urban agglomeration of the steel city of Visakhapatnam.

The Dibbapalem Rehabilitation Centre constructed in the middle of agricultural fields, north of Balacheruvu backwaters, near a hillock called *Devadakonda*, situated at a distance of about five kms. from Dibbapalem sea-shore. The Jalaris inhabit the southern part of the Rehabilitation Centre with the Pallis to the north and the Vada Balijas to the west as their neighbours. The Rehabilitation Centre has dug three wells to cater to the needs of all these three castes, one for the Jalari, another for the Palli and the third for the Vada Balija castes, respectively.

The roads in the Rehabilitation Centre are poorly constructed and unmetalled. No drainage facilities are provided within the colony. Electricity connections are provided only to some of the houses and many others do not have electricity. The tar road from Peddagantyada to Dibbapalem via Rehabilitation Centre was laid in 1983 and public transport was introduced to ply upto Dibbapalem village. Now there is an hourly direct bus service between Visakhapatnam and Dibbapalem. It has been stated that in the old village mosquitoes were uncommon.

Now in the Rehabilitation Centre mosquitoes are abundant perhaps due to climatic changes and poor drainage facilities. They also complain that there are many types of snakes found here, such as, cobras and krait. It has also been reported that there were two deaths due to snake bite after coming into the Rehabilitation Centre.

Medical facilities in the village are very poor. However, there is a building constructed for the Health Centre in the Rehabilitation Centre but without doctor, nurse and compounder or mid-wife. The village Jalaripalem, in its new setting, has changed considerably in its appearance. In place of disorderly erected thatched huts now stands *pucca* tiled houses constructed of bricks and cement in a planned manner. Each new building constructed on a 107 square yards plot consists of a living room, kitchen and a small verandah. The interior of the village has changed little except for the introduction of street lights.

The Rehabilitation Centre has a school upto seventh class catering to the needs of the children belonging to the Jalari, Palli and Vada Balija castes. The school is housed in a *pucca* building, much spacious than the one in the original Jalaripalem village which was housed in a thatched house. Unlike in my first visit, now I could see several Jalari children attending the school. The Jalari parents are showing keen interest in educating their children as they consider the steel plant as a provider of jobs and sending the children to the school is worth of it.

The present Headmaster of the school is Allam Krishna Murthy who has been a teacher in Gangavaram Samiti since 1979. The other teacher is Ramayya who has been a teacher in Jalaripalem primary school since 1965. It is very heartening to note that almost all the Jalari children are attending the school regularly and the parents are taking considerable interest in sending their children to school. This was not the case during my previous visit in 1969.

In 1969, in general, all the Jalari fathers expected their sons to help them in fishing. Even the younger children below ten years of age were not spared. These boys had specified jobs to attend to when the fishing boats and catamarans landed on the beach. Even those few who then were attending the primary school were expected to help their fathers and take up fishing on completing twelve years of age. Now with a changed situation, when fishing has been giving way to wage labour and other alternative job opportunities, the Jalari parents are willing to invest in their children's education.

Another conspicuous feature most prominent is the change in dress pattern of the Jalaris. In place of a loin cloth around their waist, the

Jalari boys now-a-days are wearing pants and shirts. Men and women are now supporting colourful dresses instead of red colour which was the only favourite colour for them. Young girls and women are invariably wearing colourful blouses which used to be a feature only of a few well-to-do households in 1969.

RELIGIOUS LIFE

Religious life of the Jalaris did not undergo much change. The Jalaris still maintain very close contacts with their Palli neighbours in matters related to the village festival. They perform rituals together for the village deities. The centre of the village for religious activities (*grama sadanu*), which is situated by the side of the Chinthapilli Sattayya's house, is used as a meeting place for both the Jalaris and Pallis of *Peddametta* and *Chinnametta* to discuss matters related to the performance of ceremonies and rituals to the village goddesses.

After coming to the Rehabilitation Centre the Jalaris and Pallis have installed goddesses of the village to the east of their new settlement, as it was in the original village of Jalaripalem, near Devakonda hillock. They had celebrated the village festival on a grand scale on *dola punnami* in May 1985. They collected a total of Rs. 15,000 by way of donations from each household of the Palli and Jalari castes. Every household contributed Rs. 60 each. They have worshipped the village goddesses, viz. *Peddammavaru, Poleramma, Nukallamma, Durgalamma* and *Rasa Muthyalamma*. They have sacrificed goats and hen to all these village goddesses, except the last mentioned deity, as *Rasa Muthyalamma* does not like to have blood and sacrifices as offerings but accepts only fruits and coconuts. The chief worshipper (*pedda dasudu*) was Erabala Gurappa of the Palli caste. Kasarapu Tatayya of Jalari caste is next in hierarchy to perform the rituals to the village goddesses.[1] This is the first village festival celebrated by the Jalaris and Pallis together as they were doing in their original village of Jalaripalem.

For the village festival, the lineage priests (*dasullu*) from Chinthapilli and Kasarapu lineages took the lead and celebrated the festival. Food was served to all belonging to Jalaripalem. It was estimated that Rs. 10,000 was spent on that day's celebration as it was the first village festival celebrated in the Rehabilitation Centre. Chinthapilli Sattayya played a leading role in this celebration and all the other lineage priests also participated. Rice, meat and chicken were cooked and served on that night. Every Jalari was neatly dressed and was in high spirits. A drama troupe was called from Srikakulam and a drama on *Pandava Vijayam* was performed. This cost the villagers Rs. 800. Procession was taken out around the village. All the procedures were carefully followed in the performance of ritual and distribution of food, as they said, any mistake in the procedures would have made the participants boycott the celebrations.

The Jalaris, after coming to Dibbapalem Rehabilitation Centre, found an idol in the nearby Devadadonda hillock from a cave. This idol was brought down to the foothills of the hillock. It resembles a herostone but the sex of the statue is difficult to determine. The people are worshipping the idol as a male God and have named it *swamvaru,* meaning the supreme god. There is also a spring found coming from the top of the hill. But its origin is not known. People regard the spring as sacred. The water tastes sweet and people use it for drinking purposes. This water is available throughout the year.

Every lineage in the Rehabilitation Centre has its own separate Peddillu constructed on 105 square yards plot allotted by Revenue Department. Ritual activity on the domestic front also shows continuity in the form, but changes in the content. Inner lineages of the households of brothers still perform ancestor worship to their immediate ancestor, but their composition differs from those in 1969. Kambala Bhooloka who was hitherto performing rituals to his dead father and the other ancestors, along with his elder brother, has now separated from him after coming to the Rehabilitation Centre. The inner lineage of Kambala Bhooloka acts as an independent unit of his own, consisting of himself and his four sons, performs ancestor worship periodically to his dead father and other ancestors, independent of his elder brother and his sons. Similarly, I have observed that many of the brothers who were performing common rituals hitherto to their ancestors, now have formed independent inner lineages of their own.

Christian missionary activity is seen in the Rehabilitation Centre. Mr. Allam Krishna Murthy, a former teacher of the school in Gangavaram village, is the missionary. The faith spread among the Vada Balija and a few are converted to Christianity. The Rehabilitation Centre has a church. Allam Krishna Murthy's missionary work is ably supported by Eripilli Apparao and Perla Nallayya who have been helping him in his work. It is also reported that a girl aged 20 is planning to become a nun.

POLITICAL DEVELOPMENTS

There are several changes noticed in the structure of the village administration from my first visit to Jalaripalem. Jalaripalem was a constituent village of Nellimukku *panchayat* when I first visited the village in 1969. Later a separate village *panchayat* of Gangavaram was constituted consisting of the fisherman villages of Gangavaram, Jalaripalem, Peddametta and Chinnametta. Maidi Raja Rao, a Vada caste man of Gangavaram, was elected president and Erabala Tatabbai, a Palli of Pedametta, was elected vice president in 1969.

Elections were conducted in 1984 after the constituent villages of Gangavaram *panchayat*, namely, Gangavaram, Jalaripalem, Peddametta and Chinnametta, were shifted to Dibbapalem Rehabilitation Centre and its establishment as a separate *panchayat*. During the *panchayat* elections, contest was mainly confined to the Vadas only. The contest for the post of president of the *panchayat* was between the two Vada candidates, viz., Eripilli Apparao and Maidi Rajeswara Rao, son of the late Raja Rao, who was the first president of Gangavaram *panchayat*. Maidi Rajeswara Rao was defeated in the elections and Eripilli Appa Rao was elected as president. The lone representative Chintapilli Appalaswamy from Jalaripalem was elected unopposed as *panchayat* member. However, Chintapilli Sattayya was later elected unopposed after the death of his father Appalaswamy who was made vice president.

The caste *panchayat* is still functioning as it was in 1969, but with changes in the leadership. The village is administered by the headman of the existing ten lineages in the village representing their respective lineages. They are : (1) Kasarapu Sattayya, (2) Kadiri Appanna, (3) Kantumuchchu Tatayya, (4) Chinthapilli Sattayya, (5) Kantumuchchu Nukayya, (6) Karaku Nallayya, (7) Modu Appanna, (8) Nolli Bhooloka, (9) Vadamodilli Bhooloka and (10) Kambala Bhooloka.

The Jalaris now recognize Kasarapu Sattayya as the traditional leader of the Jalaris though he ranks second after the Kadiri lineage head. Whereas Kadiri Appanna, son of the late Kadiri Krishnamurthy, the traditional village head during my first visit, the next important leader is relegated to a second position. Kambala Bhooloka and Chinthapilli Sattayya are the other influential traditional leaders in the village.

Kadiri Appanna who could have been the traditional head of the village is mild and unassuming, unlike his father Kadiri Krishnamurthy. The traditional leadership now lost its hold of political power over the village and submitted its powers to the elected leader of the *panchayat* Chinthapilli Sattayya, the vice president. However, Kambala Bhooloka, the traditional leader, is influential, as he was before, with added dimension of enhanced economic status with a steady income from his two sons employed in the steel plant.

The most significant change was observed in the leadership pattern of the village. Kadiri Appanna succeeded his father Krishnamurthy, the headman of the village, who was the most influential person in the village in 1969, on his death. However, Kadiri Appanna remained only a representative of his lineage, but could not become the headman of the village. It is Chinthapilli Sattayya, the elected representative and vice president of the *panchayat*, who is usually considered by the people as the head of the village. In other words, the headmanship ceased to exist with the death of Kadiri Krishnamurthy as his son did not assert himself. It is interesting to note that the leader of Kasarapu lineage in 1969, Kasarapu Tatayya has become *bhaktudu* the lineage priest, after his elder brother's death.

The Jalaris say openly that they do not have any factions. But my brief stay suggested that Kadiri Appanna heavily depends upon Kambala Bhooloka and Kasarapu Tatayya for advice and support forming a faction against Kasarapu Sattayya and Chinthapilli Sattayya. In other words, the traditional leadership is divided and the political power from Kadiri Appanna and Kasarapu Tatayya (the traditional leader in 1969) has passed to the elected members Chinthapilli Sattayya and Kasarapu Sattayya.

ECONOMIC ORGANISATION

Fishing activity on a large scale has come down significantly in the present village. Neither catamarans nor nets are seen in its vicinity. Activities related to fishing have become less conspicuous. Most of the Jalaris have expressed a desire to sell away their nets, catamarans and boats. The reason attributed for this was the distance of the beach from the present settlement. They informed me that they are finding it difficult to go to the beach carrying the catamarans and nets on their shoulders, a distance of nearly four kilometres, for launching the craft in the sea. They are also afraid of snakes and wild animals during these operations in the night.

The Dibbapalem beach does not provide any shelter to their

property, i.e., nets and boats, and there is no security for their precious little. However, the backwaters of Balacheruvu and its surroundings provide ample opportunites for fishing with *visuru vala* (cast-net) to catch fish such as *bontalu* (mullets) and *jellalu* (cat fish), etc. These fish varieties have good market value in the industrial town of Visakhapatnam. Every Jalari who goes for fishing in the backwaters earns on an average around Rs. 10 per day. I have seen most of the youngsters in the village fishing in the backwaters.

On the other hand, the middle aged men and women are going for wage labour in the steel plant construction whenever there is work. Each man is paid Rs. 13 for a day's work by the private contractors whereas a woman is paid Rs. 10 only. Some of the Jalari women are engaged in selling fish in the nearby markets and they supplement the household economy by another Rs. 10 or so. Women and young girls are also involved in collection of firewood which they sell in the nearby market and can earn to an extent of Rs. 10 each.

The village has not abandoned big-net fishing activity completely. They have five big-nets still in use belonging to the Kasarapu, Kantumuchchu (senior), Kadiri Chinthapilli and Karuku lineages. Big-net fishing is not in use among the Modu and Kantumuchchu (junior) lineages as they had to abandon the big-net fishing activity due to lack of necessary manpower. The number of working fishermen belonging to these lineages has dwindled considerably due to demographic changes as well as new economic opportunites and other occupational alternative like wage labour. However, Modu and Kantumuchchu lineages did not sell away the big-nets and were still keeping the nets and boats with them.

The Jalaris recalled that in the old village of Jalaripalem they were happy with a steady income by way of fishing. In the evenings, hearths in all the houses were used to be lit and cooking was done. But now-a-days in the Rehabilitation Centre very few houses lit their hearths They are nostalgic about their past. It has been described as follows: In the original village only those who do not own nets used to go for share-cropping. The fish catch used to be divided into three parts. One part to the boat owner and the remaining two parts were to be divided equally among the crew. There were no mechanised fishing boats. Now they have come but fish catch has been educed. In the old village there used to be plenty of surplus fish catch which was dried up and taken in lorries to far off places in Orissa to sell. Those Jalari traders used to come back in 10 days after selling the fish with plenty of money. They agree that the share cropping is totally absent now and wage labour has given rise to uncertainties in their earnings. This change has effects on socio-economic and psychological conditions of the Jalaris.

The Jalaris are of the opinion that fish catch had increased during 1969 onwards and there was a fall in the catch after coming to the Rehabilitation Centre. Now the market value of the fish has increased and fishing in general fetches very good returns. Now the Jalaris have shifted from cotton to nylon nets which they call *silkola*. Since 1974, when the fisheries department had supplied nylon thread on subsidy, prawns were caught plentiful in the nylon nets. The nets that are in use along with the *silkola* nets are *peddolola, kavalola, isurola* and *oddivola*. Nylon net is used to fish within 40 km. in the sea. The cost of each catamaran has gone upto Rs. 4,000 each. Unlike the Vada Balijas, they do not go for *gelapu tadu* (hooks and lines) fishing. A catamaran of a bigger size with sails is worth Rs. 20,000 now.

All these developments have brought significant changes in the relations of production in fishing. Now there are no share croppers. The category of share croppers has entirely disappeared. Most of them have become wage labourers. Whatever net-groups are there, they are organised by joint households and their family members constitute the crew.

The few net groups, including big net groups that were active in the village, have been organised by the owners of the craft and tackle. The owners who have control over the nets and boats and the net groups get one third of a day's catch as rent which keeps them fairly rich with significant savings. Whereas, the daily fishing activity of *kavalola* and *silkola* organised by the family members keep them above subsistence level. It has been recorded that each individual earns Rs. 20 on average. It is also observed that none of the women folk of these households engage in selling fish.

Household economy and its viability in the original village of Jalaripalem was sustained entirely by marine fishing and its related activities whereby household used to function and maintain itself as a separate and independent economic unit. Now-a-days the sustenance of the household economy is not entirely by marine fishing and its related activities, such as selling fish in the nearby markets. Fishing in backwaters and wage labour in the construction work of the steelplant have become two major other sources of income for household economy. In place of economic contracts and arrangements for forming net groups which make the household a viable production unit, the Jalari depends now upon his labour. An average Jalari male earns his livelihood not by participating in the net groups as owner fisherman or as sharecropper, but as a wage labourer working in the construction work of the steel plant.

STANDARDS OF LIVING

The living standards of the Jalari are very low in the new situation of displacement and rehabilitation when the Jalari peasant has been transformed into the status of a wage labourer. The earnings of most of the Jalaris are meagre, barely sufficient for the subsistence of one's family. The example of Kantumuchchu Ramana, wage labourer in the construction work in the steel plant, under a private contractor, provides an example of the living conditions of the Jalari. He earns Rs. 15 a day for six days in a week and spends more than what he earns towards the household expenditure. However, the extra expenditure is met with the earnings of his wife. His wife supplements the household earnings by selling firewood collected from the nearby hillock once in a week. His family consists of his wife and two children.

The household of Vadamodali Appanna, a fisherman in the backwaters, provides another example. He earns Rs. 10 by fishing in the backwaters. Another Rs. 10 is supplemented by his wife by selling fish in the local market. The income of the household is just enough for survival.

The other economic category consists of few Jalari households having control over net groups. Their incomes mainly depend on the rent derived on them. They are definitely in a better position than the wage labourers. Their women folk do not go for wage labour.

Going in for construction work in the steel plant is still not looked upon as a source of livelihood by several Jalaris. Most of the Jalaris expressed the desire to have their settlement nearer to the beach to continue their age old tradition of marine fishing. Whereas, most of the youngsters expressed a strong desire for employment in the steel plant.

Very few fishermen in Dibbapalem Rehabilitation Centre were employed in the steel plant despite the declared preference for the displaced persons in the steel plant in matters of employment. Reason given is that an average Jalari is an illiterate and hence unsuitable for employment even for class IV jobs in the steel plant. A minimum of pass in the seventh class is required for class IV employment of a peon and khalasi. However, there are only two exceptions in this regard Kambala Bhooloka's two sons were employed in the steel plant as attenders as they have studied upto seventh class.

Each household roughly spends about 80 per cent of its income towards food and other basic necessities. The remaining amount is spent on health care, performance of ceremonies and rituals in the family. There is a conspicuous change in the food habits of the Jalari. I found during my first visit in 1969 that the Jalari depended mostly on ragi and millet and occasionally on rice and to a large extent on fish for their food. Now-a-days fish has become a rare item in their menu causing nutritional deficiencies. Previously the Jalaris were in the habit of eating *ambali*, ragi malt, but now-a-days they are using rice frequently with its gruel and porridge as staple food. The consumption of fish has come down considerably as many of them have to buy fish in the market just like any others.

FAMILY STRUCTURE VARIATIONS

The structure of the household composition shows significant variations from my earlier study conducted in 1969. The simple family structures which include single member households, two member households, broken families and nuclear families constitute only 54.54 per cent in 1969, whereas it is 71 per cent during the present study period. The extended family structures were 22.08 per cent in 1969, whereas it is only 19 per cent at present. The joint family structures, on the other hand, were 23.3 per cent in 1969 and only 10 per cent at present. Thus as we see, a considerable decrease is noted in the extended family and joint family structures. These differences can be attributed to the changes that took place during the past 18 years, especially socio-economic changes, due to the displacement and rehabilitation.

Although it was not possible for me to conduct a survey of all the 240 Jalari households in the Dibbapalem Rehabilitation Centre; yet, I was able to conduct census survey very briefly for 80 households only, taken as a representative sample, to understand the trends of change in the household structures and their composition. An analysis of the household composition reveals distribution of categories of household structures: (Table 6.1)

Table 6.1: Classification of Family Structures in 1985

Type of family	*No. of households*	*Percentage*
Simple family structures	57	71
Extended family structures	15	19
Joint family structures	8	10

There are several variations found in the genealogical composition of the simple family structures. Majority of these structures consists of a man, his wife and children. However, there are a few households consisting of a man and his wife only. Some of these cases are of married couple living separately and the others are of the couples having married children who had separated from them.

There are also cases of incomplete nuclear families without a male head and a woman living along with her children. For example Kadiri Mutyalamma (50) is living with her only son (21) who is mentally retarded and suffers epilepsy fits. There is one single woman household of Kantumuchchu Bhoolokamma, a widowed woman (55) living alone. Her married sons are living separately but help her with money regularly.

The other household consists of a widowed woman (25) named Nolli Bhoolokamma, her son (six) and a daughter (four). The husband of the woman died in 1982. Another household consists of a young widow Karaku Nallamma (20) and her two-year old daughter. Her husband also died of malaria when they moved into the new settlement in october 1982. Modu Bhoolokamma (40) lives with her two daughters. Her husband also died of malaria three years ago. She earns her livelihood by going as wage labourer for construction work in the steel plant.

The genealogical composition of the extended family structures includes the primary unit of a nuclear family consisting of a man, his wife and children with dependent kinsmen, such as a widower (father) or widow (mother) and/or unmarried siblings. The analysis of the cases of the formation of the extended family structures reveals two significant processes. They are: one, simple extension takes place to the nuclear family structure by inclusion of a dependent member such as, a widower (father) or mother or brother and/or sister. For example, the household of Kadiri Gurappa (38) consists of his wife, son and his widower (father) (65). Whereas, the household of Chinthapilli Tata

(42) consists of his widowed mother (62) besides his wife and children.

Though majority of the extended households studied belongs to this category, the remaining household structures reveal the inclusion of a widower (father) or widow (mother) with dependent siblings. For example in the genealogy of the household of Kantumuchchu Gurrayya (45) it was found that the extension took place with the inclusion of the widowed mother (65) and her adopted son (18).

Other interesting patterns and still complex structures have also been observed in several households. The household of Karaku Nallanna is illustrated below. Karaku Nallanna (58) is residing with his wife, two unmarried sons and a daughter along with his widowed daughter-in-law and her daughter. His eldest son died due to malaria soon after moving into the Rehabilitation Centre leaving his wife and daughter to the care of his father. The household of Kadiri Danayya (35) serves yet another example. It consists of his wife and two children along with the dependent widowed mother (70) and a dependent widowed elder sister (58). The household of Modu Sattayya (25), besides his wife and a child, also includes his widowed grand-mother (60) and her dependent widowed daughter who is physically handicapped.

The household structure of Modu Sattayya includes a widowed father (60), his unmarried elder son (25) and his married younger son (20) and his wife. The household of Chintapilli Appanna consists of himself (55), his wife, two unmarried daughters and a dependent niece (BD). From the above cases we can conclude that the Jalari family has undergone significant changes during the last 18 years due to displacement, demographic and other changes of existential conditions. Unlike in 1969, the Jalari did not condemn or disapprove the inclusion of an affine into one's household. In fact, the number of dependents such as mother's mother, father-in-law and sister's daughter and widowed sister has increased and such an inclusion is treated as normal now.

The number of joint family structures has come down considerably to a mere 10 per cent. They are the households belonging to a few well-to-do Jalaris having control over big-net groups and other sources of steady incomes. The household composition of the joint family structures shows variation as it was in 1969. It was found that all the eight joint households recorded in the sample belong to Kadiri, Kasarapu, Kantumuchchu (senior), Chintapilli and Kambala lineages. The genealogical composition of some of these joint family structures are discussed below :

The household of Kadiri Appanna (48) consists of Appanna, his wife (42) and dependent children and the family of his married son (25). The household of Kasarapu Tatayya (58) consists of the families of Tatayya and his brother (55). The composition of the household of Kantumuchchu Yellayya (60) consists of Yellayya, his unmarried children along with his married son (35) and daughter-in-law.

The sample also includes two other significant joint household structures. They are the households of Kambala Bhooloka, his second son Masena Tata and Kadiri Kistayya. Kambala Bhooloka's household consists of Kambala Bhooloka (55), his wife and his three married sons and their respective families. His first son Gurayya (35) is living with his father and has no children. His third and fourth sons, Chenchu Tata (29) and Nallayya (26) are also living with their father in a joint household setting. Chenchu Tata has a wife and a daughter. The second son Masenu Tata (32) has a wife and three daughters and is living separately with his father-in-law (61). The other joint household belongs to Kadiri Kistayya (75) which includes his wife, his son's daughter (23), her husband and their three daughters. So this is an *illarikam* household.[2] The husband of Kadiri Kistayya's son's daughter came into the household of his wife and was living permanently after marriage. It should be noted that Kadiri Kistayya's SDH (son's daughter's husband) is, in fact, his daughter's son. His son's daughter (SD) married her father's sister's son (FSS).

Household of Kambala Bhooloka is very fortunate as employment of his two sons in the steel plant as attenders gives it a steady income. The household consists of his wife, three sons and their respective families. They live in a house built on 428 square yards allotted to the father and sons. It is a spacious house with electrical fittings. Though Kadiri Bhooloka and his sons are living together under the same roof, each nuclear family cooks its own food separately and has its separate hearth. However, their incomes are given to the father who is the head of the household and he distributes the money to the sons according to their needs. This type of joint family organization is new to Jalaripalem and this new system has been adopted by Kambala Bhooloka in a new situation of economic opportunities and expansion. The sons under the guardianship of their father pool their incomes and live under one roof but cook and eat separately. One of the essential elements of a joint family, i.e., commensality, is absent in this case but it retained other features: common property and income, co-residence and common worship.

It was noted in my previous study that joint household was the most favoured type of family structure both as an idelogy and practice. The joint family organization is still a dominant theme among the Jalaris and is an ideal pattern. As a value it is maximised by all the Jalaris. Commensality and co-residence, followed by common property, common income and common worship were the significant features symbolising joint family organization among the Jalaris in 1969. Now some of these features are not emphasized and they are rearranged in a hierarchical order of relative significance. Common income and co-residence is emphasized over all other features, whereas, commensality, and common property became less important.

In the realm of family relations significant changes have also been noticed. The agnatic emphasis, though still dominant, has accommodated the affinal relationships in matters of household composition. The relations between affines have become more stronger by increased interaction in the domestic sphere, though the agnatic emphasis still retains its stronghold with frequent common religious activities.

A resident of Dibbapalem has a rice mill on the southern side of the Rehabilitation Centre. He runs a video film show every day in the evenings by charging Rs. 1.50 per head. These shows are very popular with the women and the children of Jalaripalem. It was told that he shows the latest Telegu movies. It is gathered that occasionally he also shows blue films and this has an adverse effect on the family relationships of the Jalaris, especially between the wife and husband.

CONTINUITY AND CHANGE

Though the Jalaris have changed considerably consequent upon displacement and rehabilitation they have retained several of their cultural features. The chages that are very conspicuous belong to the realm of social structural reality. On the other hand, cultural repertoire such as, the concepts, jural norms, ideas related to the family organization belonging to the realm of cultural dimension, has not changed much. Changes brought about by displacement and rehabilitation have made them to adapt to the new ecological setting, different from the one in the original village. This has brought about the adjustments in the patterns of livelihood and living conditions.

Due to the distance of the sea from the Rehabilitation Centre, fishing activity has come down considerably and gave way to new modes of living. The opportunities that were offered by the backwaters for fishing were being utilized by some. Whereas, others have utilized the opportunities provided by the construction work in the steel plant and have become wage labourers. The Devadakonda hillock on the northern side of the Rehabilitation Centre has also provided opportunities for the women and girls to collect firewood to earn to the extent of Rs. five to ten per day.

The changes in the nature of mode of production have affected the relations of family structure to a large extent whereas the importance of joint family in practice has decreased and the relative importance of nuclear family has emerged. However, it is noteworthy to point out that the Jalaris still adhere to the set of ideas, concepts, rules and strategies related to the family and its organisation as they were in the original village. They still consider that joint living is superior to separate living despite the conditions favouring the latter. Then attention was drawn to the fact of difference between the structure of joint living in 1969 and 1985 and functioning of the joint household of Kadiri Bhooloka was cited as an example of change.

Kadiri Bhooloka and three of his married sons are living together under the same roof but have separate dwellings of their own. They are pooling their incomes but are having separate and independent budgets. Now the important feature of joint living in 1969, i.e., commensality, is conspicuously absent in this joint setting. However, this has been defended by the Jalaris. They said that each nuclear family had its separate needs and requirements different from the other and, therefore, each nuclear family should be allowed to have its own budget.

They say that joint living is to be considered from a single feature, that is, living under one roof. Other features, such as, common property and common hearth, are secondary because of change in social conditions. The arrangement of these features is contextual. In other words, what the Jalaris are trying to convey is that though the social structural reality of the households has changed due to the changes in the existential conditions, the cultural values, norms and ideas related to the family organization have not changed, but re-arranged. They still adhere to the same values and ideas and try to give a form and meaning to the existing pattern of family organisation which is re-interpreted by these values and ideas.

REFERENCES

1. Kasarapu Tatayya was the lineage head during my first visit to Jalari in 1969 and his elder brother was the lineage priest.
2. *Illarikam* is a custom of post-marital residence of the man with his wife's household.

SEVEN

CONCLUSIONS

IN the preceding chapters we have discussed various aspects of the cultural and social structural dimensions of the Jalari family and household such as cultural codes, as manifested in the values, beliefs and concepts, genealogical composition of the households, and rules and strategies. It should now be possible for us to draw conclusions on the major features of the preceding description and analysis. This will be done in the following summary :

The Jalari household (*illu*) is the basic and the most discrete kin group among the Jalaris. The variation in genealogical composition of the households cannot be construed as exhibiting different stages of the developmental cycle in domestic groups in a lineal order. Not all the Jalari households pass through the various phases from a nuclear household to a joint household. Some households are fitted into the pattern and some do not correlate. The differential occurrence of genealogical pattern in the household composition among the Jalaris reflects the Jalari's different resources, his efforts to maximise self-interests, to develop his private assets in an arena of culturally defined constraints and incentives. Each Jalari household grows and develops in time as a consequence of decisions the married males take in the context of events such as birth, marriage and death.

The members of the family, who are genealogically related to each other as parents, sons and siblings, on the other hand, are culturally bound together by 'codes of conduct' as revealed in the concepts, beliefs and ideas related to the membership into the family through the medium of 'incorporation'. Such a membership involves a number of rites and rituals that have meanings connecting the individuals with each other through the 'codes of conduct'.

The Jalari family, however, is not simply a genealogical construct, but also a cultural construct. This has been demonstrated, as noted before, in the various stages of transition of the Jalari from his birth to death. For example, the transition of a new born child from a state of pollution to ritual purity and to its social environment does not automatically confer it with a membership into the family in which it is born. The social significance of the new born child is recognised only when it is ritually named and formally 'incorporated' into the family and the social acceptance of the child with its father, mother, kinsmen and ancestors is ceremonially recognised and established.

Parents perform rituals for the well-being of their children. The last important duty a father owes to a child is the performance of its marriage. In fact, a child has the right to demand from its parents to arrange for its marriage.

On the other hand, the 'codes of conduct' for a son includes his obligations due to his family, such as, to look after his household, his parents in their old age and his dependent siblings. It also includes the performance of the last rites and ceremonies to the parents, ancestors and family deities. Such obligatory performance of moral duties between parents and child not only binds them together, but also establishes a continuity between the living members and ancestors of past, present and future generations of a family. Whereas, the activities of the household as well as its organisation, cultural rules and strategies related to the household division reveal the processes of maintenance and replacement of the households in time.

We have already noted that the Jalari conceptualize the physical facts, such as birth, as related closely with the membership through the process of 'incorporation' into the family with certain 'codes of conduct'. This is based upon the belief that the newly born child's life is wholly made out of the man and, therefore, the child belongs to the man, and not to the woman.

This cultural premises of agnatic emphasis is conspicuous in the distinctions made between the positions of males and females in terms of their rights and role-expectations. Family as a model of kinship ensures sons with rights in matters of inheritance and succession. The rights of the male members of a household are recognised and given importance. Therefore, the Jalari men, as inheritors of property, are important to family, while the Jalari women are secondary. However, an unmarried girl or a widow has the right to maintenance in her natal household.

The significant feature of the Jalari domestic organisation is conceptual distinction people make between family (*kutumbam*) and the household (*illu*), a distinction based on the contrast between kinship and common residence as external manifestations of the same reality. Both kinship and residence are considered the essential features of the family and household, respectively, but they are logically distinct and empirically different, one belonging to the cultural dimension and the other to social-structural dimension. Once we realise that both the family and household belong to different levels of the same phenomenon, it is then possible to separate family from the household. This distinction is necessary because anthropologists have given to family a false concreteness by perceiving it as a solid group of genealogical model that exists in the real world. In fact, family, like any other kinship category, is a model which exists only as a conceptual category and the genealogical model is its external manifestation.

In fact, the Jalari term used for family (*kutumbam*) is not just a model of genealogy, but refers to a cultural model of 'codes of conduct', a set of ideas defining the relationships and other attributes. Thus, family is a symbol of the very existence of the Jalari. This model of 'codes of conduct' exists in the conceptual world of the people as a shared knowledge with which experience and action are interpreted and given structure of meaning. Though social structural reality of the households has changed due to the changes in the existential conditions, the cultural values, norms and ideas related to the family organization have not changed, but re-arranged.

Thus, family is not simply a genealogical construct but a cultural construct. The Jalaris maximize the values, interpret concepts and beliefs to give a form and meaning to the household activities and social action. They also apply and manipulate the rules and strategies for their advantage in the world of necessity as determined by the material infrastructure. All Jalaris share the same set of values, concepts, beliefs, ideas, rules and strategies on how their family is or should be arranged and organised. This shared knowledge exists on its own right and guides and restructures the reality with a form and meaning. On the other hand, the social structural dimension, in which household activities and events and transactions take place, belongs to the world of necessity which is determined by the particular ecologic, demographic and economic conditions. Both the cultural and social structural dimensions complement each other and represent the totality of conditions of production and reproduction of structures of family and household in the Jalari society.

GLOSSARY

ainillu	=	main room
akshintalu	=	rice mixed with turmeric used for blessing on auspicious occasions
ambali	=	porridge
Ammoru	=	deity
appaginthalu	=	handing over the bride to the in-laws
arapa	=	1/8 part of the big-net
ariselu	=	a sweet made of rice flour and jaggery
arugu	=	pial, raised platform adjoining the front walls of the house
atukulu	=	rice wetted, parched and flattened
Berakathelu	=	wholesale woman traders in-between the fishermen and the retail traders
Bhakthudu	=	lineage priest
Chakali	=	washerman
Chepalvallu	=	fisherman
chinnababu	=	father's younger brother
chinadinam	=	ceremony performed on the third day after death
Chinnametta	=	name of the village of the Palli and Golla castes
Dasudu	=	village priest (*dasullu* pl.)
Devadakonda	=	name of the hillock in the Rehabilitation Centre
dharmam	=	codes of conduct for moral order
diga veedhi	=	lower ward
dolapunnami	=	full moon day in the month of November
Durgalamma	=	name of the village deity
ega veedhi	=	upper ward

enalu	=	celebration marking the induction of the bride into her husband's house
gadapa thokkadam	=	induction of the girl into her husband's house
garbadhanam	=	consummation
gandham	=	paste of sandal wood
gelaputadu	=	hooks and lines
gondillu	=	place of worship
grama pedda	=	village head
grama peddalu	=	village elders
grama sadanu	=	central palce of the village
gudisillu	=	conical house
illu	=	house
Intammoru	=	family deity
intiperulu	=	surnames
irugola	=	gill-net
isurola	=	cast-net
jellalu	=	catfish
jonna	=	a cereal (jowar)
kalisivundadam	=	joint living
karavaka	=	sea-shore
Karanam	=	village accountant
katnalu	=	dowry
kanukalu	=	prestations
kavalola	=	gill-net
kavvallu	=	sardines
kayakam	=	a medicinal preparation given to post-natal mother
kottamavasa	=	new year day of Telugu calendar
kulapedda	=	caste head
kumkum	=	vermillion
kutumbam	=	family
makarasankranthi	=	festival celebrated on January 14 of each year
Mangali	=	barber
Marakathelu	=	petty traders of fish
Mantrasani	=	mid-wife
molathadu	=	a thread tied around the waist

moolakuthechuta	=	ceremonial performance to signify bringing the ancestors back to the home for worship
middillu	=	house with mud ceilings
muhurtham	=	auspicious time
melathappadam	=	cessation of monthly periods (family way)
nelavaram	=	ceremony performed a month after death
neththallu	=	white bait
oddivola	=	dragnet
oke' kunda vanta	=	cooking in the same vessel
oke' kutumbamulo	=	of the same family
paga	=	a turban to tie on or from a turban
pandari ratalu	=	pandal erected on a marriage ceremony
pandava vijayam	=	a drama depicting the victory of Pandavas
parayi sottu	=	property of others
pasupu	=	turmeric
pasupu koka	=	white *saree* of the bride dipped in turmeric water
pedda babu	=	father's elder brother
pedda dasudu	=	principal priest of the village
Pedda manisulu	=	Village elders who are influential
Peddammorlu	=	principal deity
peddola	=	seine net (big-net)
Peddillu	=	shrine of the lineage deity
peenu	=	earthen dais where marriage ritual is performed
peeta	=	a seat made of board
pellipandiri	=	marriage pandal
pelli koduku	=	bride groom
pillagadu	=	lineage head
pellipeenu	=	earthen dais where marriage ritual is performed
Poleramma	=	name of the village deity
poyyi	=	hearth
pusthe	=	marriage locket
raithu	=	share-cropper

rokali	=	wooden pestle
sare	=	gifts and presentations given at the time of puberty and marriage of a girl
Satani	=	a non-brahmin priest of vaishnava cult
sathamanam	=	marriage locket
Sammiti	=	village massenger
silkola	=	nylon net
Sonthadarudu	=	owner
Swami varu	=	the supreme god
upputeru	=	backwaters
undi	=	a system of social organisation where the village is divided into two halves
Urammorlu	=	village deity
vasillu	=	rectangular house
vavili	=	the five leaved chaste tree *vitex negundo* or *cleone pentaphylla*
veedhi	=	street
vuregimpu	=	marriage procession

BIBLIOGRAPHY

Abbi, Behari L., 'Urban Family in India' *Contribution to Indian Sociology*, 1969 (New Series) 3 : 116-127.

Bailey F.G., *Caste and the Economic Frontier :A village in Highland Orissa*, 1957 Manchester, Manchester University Press.

Barth, Fredrik, *Models of Social Organisation*, Occasional Paper (No. 23), 1966 London, Royal Anthropological Institute.

Beals, A.R., *Gopalpur*, New York, Holt, Rinehart and Winston.

Berreman, G.A., *Hindus of the Himalayas*, 1963, Berkeley and Los Angeles, University of California Press.

Census of India, *A monograph on Mofusbandar*: Part VI village survey Monographs (No. 7), 1961, Andhra Pradesh Hyderabad, Census of India.

Cohn, Bernard, 'Chamar Family in a North Indian Village', *The Economic Weekly* (13); 1051-1055, 1961.

Desai, I.P., 'An analysis In Symposium: Caste and Joint Family', *Sociological Bulletin* (4): 97-117, 1955.

Desai, I.P., 'The joint Family in India: An analysis', *Sociological Bulletin* (5): 144-156, 1956.

Desai, I.P., *Some Aspects of Family in Mahuva*, Bombay, Asia Publishing House, 1964.

Dube, S.C., *Indian Village : Ithaca*, New York Cornell University Press, 1955.

Dumont, L.P., 'Kinship and Alliance among the Kallar', *The Eastern Anthropologist* 4(1):3-26, 1950.

Dumont, L.P., 'The Dravidian Kinship Terminology as an Expression of Marriage', *Man* (53):34-39, 1953.

Dumont, L.P., *Hierarchy and Marriage Alliance in South Indian Kinship*, Occasional Papers (No. 12), London, Royal Anthropological Institute, 1957.

Dumont, L.P., 'Marriage in India: The Present State of the Question', *Contribution to Indian Sociology* (7):77-98, 1961.

Dumont, L.P., 'Marriage in India': The Present State of the Question II: Marriage and Status : *Nayar and Newar Contribution to Indian Sociology* (7):77-98, 1964.

Dumont and Pocock, (eds.) 'Village studies' and 'Kinship', *Contributions to Indian Sociology* (1) : 23-64, 1957.

Dumont and Pocock, 'For a Sociology of India: A Rejoinder to Dr. Bailey', *Contributions to Indian Sociology* (4): 82-89, 1960.

Epstein, T. Scarlet, *Economic Development and Social Change in South India*, Manchester, Manchester University Press, 1962.

Fortes, Mayer, *The Web of Kinship Among the Tallensi*, London, Oxford University Press, 1949.

Fortes, Mayer, 'Introduction', in *The Developmental Cycle in Domestic Groups*, Jack Goody (Ed.) Cambridge Papers in Social Anthropology (No. 1), Cambridge, Cambridge University Press, 1958.

Gore, M.S., 'The Husband-Wife and the Motner-Son Relationships', *Sociological Bulletin* (11):91-102, 1961.

Gore, M.S., *Urbanization and Family Change* Bombay, Popular Prakashan, 1968.

Gough, E. Kathleen, 'Changing Kinship Usages in the Setting of Political and Economic Change among the Nayars of Malabar', *Journal of the Royal Anthropological Institute* (82) 1952.

Gough, E. Kathleen, 'Brahman Kinship in a Tamil Village', *American Anthropologist* (58): 826-853, 1956.

Gough, E. Kathleen, 'The Nayars and the Definition of Marriage' *Journal of Royal Anthropological Institute* (89): 23-24, 1959.

Gough, E. Kathleen, 'Mapplla : North Kerala', in *Matri-lineal Kinship*, David M. Schneider and Kathleen Gough (Eds.):415-442 Berkeley and Los Angeles, University of California Press, 1961(a).

Gough, E. Kathleen, Nayar : Central Kerala, in *Matrilineal Kinship*, David M. Schneider and Kathleen Gough (Eds.):298-384, Berkeley and Los Angeles, University of California Press, 1961(b).

Gould, Hareld A., 'The Micro-Demography of Marriages in a North Indian Area' *Southwestern Journal of Anth-ropology* (17): 294-300, 1960.

Inden, Ronald and Ralph Nicholas, *Kinship in Bengali Culture*, Chicago, University of Chicago Press, 1977.

Kapadia, K.M., 'Rural Family Patterns', *Sociological Bulletin* (5): 111-126, 1956.

Kapadia K.M., 'The Family in Transition', *Sociological Bulletin* (8): 68-99, 1959.

Karve, Iravati, *Kinship Organization in India,* Poona, Deccan College Monograph Series (No. 11), 1953.

Karve, Iravati, 'Caste in Modern Times', *Report of the Seminar on Castism* : Bombay, 1956.

Klass, Morton, 'Marriage Rules in Bengal', *American Anthropologist* (68) 951-970, 1966.

Kutty, A.R., *Marriage and Kinship in an Island Society*, University of Saugar Monographs (No. 2), Delhi National Publishing House, 1972.

Lewis, Oscar, *Village Life in Northern India : Studies in a Delhi Village*, Urbana, University of Illinois Press, 1958.

Lynch, Owen, *The Politics of Untouchability, Social Mobility and Social Change in City of India*, New York, Columbia University Press, 1969.

Madan, T.N., 'Is the Brahmanic Gotra a Grouping of Kin?', *Southwestern Journal of Anthropology 18* (1): 59-77, 1962(a).

Madan, T.N., 'The Hindu Joint Family', *Man 62* (No. 145):88, 1962 (b).

Madan, T.N., The Joint Family: A Terminological Clarification', *International Journal of Comparative Sociology* 3(1):7-16, 1962(c).

Madan, T.N., *Family and Kinship: A Study of the Pandits of Rural Kashmir*, Bombay Asia Publishing House, 1965.

Madan, T.N., 'Marriage and Kinship in India : Two recent Studies', *Contributions to Indian Sociology* (7):135-143, 1973.

Majumdar, D.N., *Caste and Communication in an Indian Village*, Bombay, Asia Publishing House, 1958.

Mandelbaum, DavidSociety in India, Bombay, Popular Prakashan, 1972.

Mayer, A.C., *Caste and Kinship in Central India : A Village and its Region*, London, Routledge and Kegan Paul, 1960.

McCormack, William 'Sister-Daughter Marriage in a Mysore Village' *Man in India 58* (1): 34-48, 1958.

Murdock, George, *Social Structure*, New York, MacMillan, 1948.

Nadel, S.F., *The Foundations of Social Anthropology*, London Cohen & West, 1951.

Parry, Johanath, *Caste and Kinship in Kangra,* New Delhi Vikas Publishing House, 1979.

Pocock, David, *Kanbi and Patidar : A Study of the Patidar Community of Gujarat*, Oxford, Clarendon Press, 1972.

Radcliffe-Brown, A.R., *Structure and Function in Primitive Society*, London, Cohen and West, 1952.

Ramana, K.V., *Caste and Society in an Andhra Town*, PhD Dissertation submitted to the University of Illinois at Urbana Champaign, 1971.

Redfield, Robert, *Peasant Society and Culture*, Chicago, The University of Chicago Press, 1956.

Rivers, W.H.R., 'The Marriage of Cousins in India', *Journal of Royal Asiatic Society* : 611-640, 1907.

Rivers, W.H.R., *Kinship and Social Organisation* London, Constable, 1914.

Ross, Aileen D., *The Hindu Family in its Urban Setting*, Bombay, Oxford University Press, 1961.

Shah, A.M., *The Household Dimension of the Family in India*, New Delhi, Orient Longman, 1973.

Srinivas, M.N., *Religion and Society among the Coorg of South India*, Oxford, Oxford University Press, 1952.

Thurston, Edgar, *Castes and Tribes of Southern India*, (Vols.1:218-222; 2:442-446; 6:1-28; 7: 258-265) Madras, Government Press, 1909.

Van der Veen, Klass W., *I Give Thee My Daughter*, Assen, Van Gorcum & Co., 1972.

Vatuk Sylvia, *Kinship and Urbanization : White Collar Migrants in North India*, Berkeley and Los Angeles, University of California Press, 1972.

Yalman, Nur, *Under the Bo Tree : Studies in Caste, Kinship and Marriage in the Interior of Ceylon*, Berkeley and Los Angeles, University of California Press, 1967.

INDEX